Glimpses of Wilderness

Glimpses of Wilderness

by
Kevin Proescholdt

NORTH STAR PRESS OF ST. CLOUD, INC.
St. Cloud, Minnesota

Dedication

To Jean, BT, and all my companions
with whom I've shared glimpses of wilderness

Table of Contents

Glimpses of Wilderness

1

Glimpses of Wilderness

Wilderness has shaped and enriched my life.

I have had the good fortune of visiting a multitude of wilderness areas, from small wilderness areas like the Black Elk Wilderness in South Dakota's Black Hills to the rugged mountain wildernesses of the Rockies like the Bob Marshall Wilderness in Montana, to the beautiful alpine wilderness regions of California's Sierra Nevada Mountains. I have visited tiny wilderness areas so small they don't allow overnight camping, and I have disappeared for weeks at a time in some of the vast wild reaches of the Canadian Arctic and Alaska.

The wilderness I love best, however, is the hauntingly beautiful lakeland wilderness along the Canada-United States border in northeastern Minnesota and southern Ontario. This area, the million-acre Boundary Waters Canoe Area Wilderness and the slightly larger Quetico Provincial Park, is a fabled maze of wilderness waterways that has attracted paddlers and solitude seekers for a century or more. Here I've camped under tall pines and ancient cedars, paddled sparkling chains of lakes, and experienced the deep silences of a wild region beyond the reach of modern civilization. This wilderness is home to moose and black bear, lake trout and northern pike, the brightly colored Blackburnian warbler and the mighty bald eagle.

For a decade, I guided canoe trips throughout the Boundary Waters Wilderness, exploring the region and falling more deeply in love with the area and its wild character on every trip. I experienced the region's natural beauty, delighted in the northern lights, thrilled while exploring new lakes and new routes. I quickly became convinced that the BWCAW was worthy of the best protection possible so it could remain unspoiled and free of development for future generations.

As time went on and I had time to reflect more deeply on the Boundary Waters, I realized the area has immense value beyond just the thrill of catching a big walleye or the physical satisfaction of paddling and portaging a twenty-mile day. The Boundary Waters and Quetico, together with Voyageurs National Park and LaVerendrye Provincial Park, form the 2.5-million-acre international Quetico-Superior Ecosystem. The region possesses an enormous range of values—intrinsic and ecological values as well as the deeper intangible values that emerge from our immersion in the area's wilderness character. All these values can bring meaning to a person's life, regardless of whether that person actually visits or experiences the region first-hand.

Through the years, I have come to realize that I often experienced or sensed these deeper values through what my friend and wilderness author Sigurd Olson called "flashes of insight," those glimpses of perception or new perspective that often came while in the wilderness itself, when my mind was most receptive to the country around me. Though I could be completely absorbed by the wilderness for an entire day or a week, it was often only during these brief moments of heightened awareness that these deeper values or meanings surfaced.

Not all of my glimpses have come in the wilderness, of course. Reading and research away from the canoe country have broadened my knowledge and deepened my understanding of the wilderness, as have many discussions with others who share my passion for wilderness. But it is during my visits to this wild lakeland region that the glimpses are most vivid and most memorable.

It is only now, after decades of traveling the area on more than

150 trips, that these individual glimpses of the area's values and characteristics have collectively given me a broad sense of the full range of its values, an outline at least of the area as a whole. Each experience has brought additional detail and clarity to my view of the region. The glimpses and insights have all deepened my understanding of and appreciation for the area and its wilderness character.

And though these glimpses come from the Quetico-Superior Ecosystem, most of these insights into wilderness values hold true in other wilderness regions, as well. I have found these same common values in many of the other wildlands I have visited across North America, both those areas protected in our great National Wilderness Preservation System as well as those that remain without permanent protection.

These wilderness values bring meaning to many peoples' lives; people hunger for a connection—or reconnection—with nature, with the wild. I believe that the wilderness itself has great intrinsic value. And I have come to appreciate the symbolic values of wilderness areas like the Boundary Waters, areas full of hope and heart and idealism that are significant to many people, even to those who may never actually visit them. As the onslaught of modern civilization modifies more and more of the natural world, it is increasingly important to preserve the ever-more-rare wilderness regions like the Boundary Waters and the entire Quetico-Superior Ecosystem. And that task of preserving the area's wilderness character is far from complete.

The Boundary Waters Canoe Area Wilderness, for example, is the most popular and most visited wilderness in the national wilderness system. Over 200,000 people visit the area every year, seeking many of the same charms and values that I do. The sheer number of visitors, however, can degrade its wilderness character by trampling campsites or degrading solitude. Motorboats still whine on more than a fifth of the area's waters. Airborne pollutants contaminate the lakes. Jeeps or trucks still rumble along some wilderness portage trails, hauling motorboats from one lake to another. Development threats, like the push for copper-nickel sulfide mining at its edge, continually arise to challenge the area's wild integrity. Lax or inappropriate stewardship by the federal or state land management agencies sometimes harms the area. And climate change has already begun to impact the Boundary Waters region in ways the full extent of which we can now only guess.

Despite these challenges, the area still possesses enormous ecological value, great natural beauty and charm, and a rich wilderness character. A reservoir of wildness astride the international border, it can, with care, continue to provide these values for the citizens not only of both nations but of the entire world. With enough glimpses into its true character, we may yet have the wisdom, humility, and restraint to fully protect it as an enduring resource of wilderness, a wild, natural legacy for all generations.

Everyone may have their own glimpses of wilderness that provide them with reasons to cherish the Boundary Waters or their own special wild area. These are some of my mine, the experiences and insights that have shaped and enriched my life, peeks into the wild that I hope may also enrich the lives of others.

2

Wilderness Magic

During the summer months the canoe country is flooded with people seeking its varied charms, and the great numbers of such visitors often erode the same charms they seek. There are moments, however, even during the busiest summer months, that the perceptive paddler experiences the magic of untouched beauty and the great wilderness silences of a land untrammeled by humankind.

Such a moment came one recent afternoon when, after waiting out a rain shower, my companion and I took to the canoe to explore our lake. We had seen many canoe groups on our route and had traveled past many overused and trampled campsites. Now we had the lake to ourselves as we paddled away from our campsite. The lake lay as glass, the thick gray clouds hung low and laden still with moisture, and the far shorelines faded to a mysterious hazy blue.

We paddled the shoreline to the northwest corner of the lake, the only canoe out and about so soon after the rain. We discovered a large hidden bay, little used and seldom seen, and our canoe glided noiselessly along its shore. Here the ledges and shelves of dark gabbro rock glistened dully from the rain, here the low rounded mounds of caribou moss stood untouched and uncrushed by boot or foot. The mats of bearberry grew thick and close to the water, and the rich color of blue flag iris provided spots of royal color along the shores. We floated into a tiny marshy bay, where the moose come to feed in the weedy shallows and where the northern pike patrol.

We passed dark, brooding stands of dripping jack pine and sensed the northward stretch of this boreal forest toward the Arctic. On one rock face we found vivid evidence of the land's rugged character and its grinding facelift, where the scratches of glacial striae rose along the rock from the water's edge, each groove paralleling the others.

Throughout this entire setting pervaded the great wilderness silence, the sound of a land removed from man-made noise, with only the natural sounds of forest and water. A faint loon call reached us from far to the south, and a ruby-crowned kinglet called frenziedly from nearby in its repeated triplet call. A blue jay scolded from through the woods, and water dripped from the trees to the lake surface of perfectly mirrored reflections below. A sense of magic fell upon us and we floated wordlessly in silence. This was the wilderness spell we sought, this the wilderness so increasingly hard to find in the canoe country.

A flutter in the nearby trees caught our eyes and we paddled closer across a shallow, sandy bay, the ripples in the sand below undisturbed by footprints or keel marks. We spotted a couple of the birds there, a small downy woodpecker flitting from tree to tree and a larger gray-and-white Canada jay that floated in and flew off soundlessly.

The climax of our afternoon exploration came as we neared some bedrock at water's edge. There we heard a soft squeaking among the fractured rock and spied a family of mink, two adults and three kits. The young had not yet fully grown; all wore a rich, dark brown coat with a white throat spot. The adults soon moved off with their characteristically graceful, fluid motion into the rock and away from our sight, and two of the kits followed closely behind.

The third young mink had become separated from the others, however, and attempted to squeeze under and through a shoreline ledge to rejoin the others. The kit appeared unafraid or unaware of us, and we had drifted at one point to within four feet of it busily negotiating its rocky obstacle. It investigated every nook and cranny with its lithe body, always on the search and never stopping for an instant. Finally it slithered around the interfering ledge just inches from the water, appearing reluctant to forsake the rock for a swim. It disappeared in the rocks with the others, just as a beaver made a huge warning splash at our sighting from just farther down the shore.

The scampering mink family a paddle's length away culminated our quest for the wilderness magic we sought this afternoon, a spell woven from more than just wildlife and quiet. The spell was concocted from a sense of remoteness and solitude and the vast wilderness silences, from the great natural beauty of an unmarred and untamed land. These things and more had combined for the special experience we felt. The enchantment remains yet in the Boundary Waters, though one must often search for it more diligently now during the summer season.

In another moment human voices reached us from far down the still lake, and the spell was broken. We turned our canoe and paddled back to camp.

3

Gabbling of Geese

We paddled west down a long canoe country lake as the darkening night gathered in around us. A waxing gibbous moon had broached the southern shoreline ridge. Although still several days to full, the moon gave us some welcome illumination. My wife Jean and I paddled steadily onward, covering the miles as the stars sparkled over us and the far western sliver of sky darkened to night.

Then, off to our right, a sudden commotion caught our attention. A yelping of many voices—no, a gabbling from many throats—broke the stillness of the evening. A flock of geese, low over the lake, circling and whirling, suddenly broke above the tree line. We could see them now, rising uncertainly, silhouettes against the night sky. Gabbling still, they formed a ragged formation and flew off out of sight or sound. It was autumn, October, and these night fliers were on their long migration south.

We had paddled a long loop route this day, exploring for the first time a string of four remote lakes that lies off from the regular travel route. All in all, we visited nearly a dozen lakes and covered about twenty miles on this lovely fall day. Sunshine had warmed the air nicely, and last night's snow-laden gusts had relaxed today to a gentle westerly breeze.

We had missed the peak of autumn's colors by a week or more, though the yellows and golds of aspen and birch still hung on in some stands quite vividly, and even in most others a ragged fringe of color remained. Tamaracks had turned yellow in the swamps, yet another two weeks until they sported a burnished gold. In some places, a few lone maples still held their brilliant colors of flaming red or eye-riveting mauve. The towering white pines that graced the forest's canopy added a rich green to the scene. The darker green of spruce seemed quite dense compared to the nearly bare stands of white birch trunks devoid of leaves.

We began the morning through a series of long, narrow lakes and the rugged topography of ridges and cliffs. The narrow neck of one lake curved past a cliffside that rose up from the water in a steep forested slope, past bare, sheer rock faces to the cliff-top high above. Atop the cliff, tall pines brushed the sky.

We left the commonly traveled route and portaged up to a long lake nestled between ridgelines. The clear, icy waters ran deep, and we wished for fishing gear to try for the lake trout we knew must be there. We carried the canoe and packs up to a smaller lake situated above the first, and stopped for a bite of lunch to survey the scene. The lake now bore the name of a mining prospector who once worked a silver claim on the lake.

We portaged higher, climbing yet another ridge on a barely discernible trail. The leaf-strewn path wound through the trees and up the slope. Fallen leaves littered the entire forest floor and made following the largely unused trail even more difficult. Then the trail began zigzagging down an even steeper slope, finally emerging at a small, remote lake.

We had wanted to reach this remote spot to get the feel of working physically hard to reach a relatively difficult backcountry lake. We had done that and more, but the most physically challenging part lay up ahead.

We crossed the small lake to its far shore and surveyed the scene. Our map showed yet another small lake beyond. No path to it existed, so we loaded our gear and "crashed" through the woods, as I like to call it, bushwhacking our way through to the next lake. Within a few rods, I spied the spot of blue through the balsam and cedar. Our route plunged downhill, where we dodged deadfalls and clambered up and over brush with the canoe. Soon we neared the shore and finally broke through the shoreline brush to set the canoe down in water once more. We quickly pushed out, hot and breathing heavily from our scramble.

We paddled across this one and began scouting for a way out, as this lake had no portages in or out. By consulting the map and surveying the shores and ridges, we decided on the most likely route. Again we crashed through the woods, up a short ridge and then down a steep slope on the other side. Soon we saw the spot of blue through the forest below, telling us we neared the large lake beyond. Before long, we arrived. Autumn color greeted us here along the far shore.

We stopped for a side hike to find a small waterfall hidden up a stream in the fall forest. We walked leisurely along the trail, noticing large moose tracks, fresh droppings, and the fall finery of the forest floor. The waterfall itself was striking, a twenty-foot drop into a pool that in summer would make an ideal swimming hole. Sun had left the waterfall by the time we arrived. A chill in the air reminded us to push on.

We backtracked to our canoe, portaged a never-ending climb over ridges, and reached the next lake two-thirds of a mile later. Then on we paddled into the setting sun, the darkening sky, the quiet night. We paddled via silhouettes and shadows, by moonlight and night vision into the cooling autumn evening. The unexpected rendezvous with the gabbling geese marked the highlight of our long paddle home that night, an encounter touched with autumn wilderness magic found best in the Quetico-Superior canoe country.

4

Opening the Canoe Country

For several years I had wanted to explore the Barto Creek country, a virtually unknown and unvisited area in the Boundary Waters Canoe Area Wilderness. The area contains no travel routes, no marked portages, and no campsites. In all my years of guiding wilderness trips in the canoe country, I had never yet worked my way into the remote Barto Creek area. Now, in early May with the high waters of spring and a crew of four other seasoned paddlers, my opportunity had finally arisen. Our expedition shoved off in two canoes with soaring spirits and a sense of adventure.

The canoe country sparkled freshly now, just after the melt. The ice had broken up a scant four days earlier; the snow had all but disappeared except for small remnants of the great winter drifts. The granite shoreline gleamed brightly in the sun, scrubbed clean by the winter snow and ice. The sunlight danced and glittered on the open water.

Leaves had not yet unfolded, and the landscape presented a study of soft, subdued hues. A pale green from the budding aspen brushed the ridges and shorelines. The swelling buds of the white-trunked birch cast a purple flush amid the aspen pastel. The muted browns of fallen leaves and dried grasses rimmed the shorelines. Only the darker greens of spruce and pine had remained rich and vivid through the long winter.

We leisurely explored the chain of lakes that first day as if seeing it for the first time. We were the first to cross the portages this spring; only last fall's aspen leaves and recent moose tracks had touched the trails before us. So early was our trip that perhaps no other person was traveling in all those million acres around us. We felt akin to the hardy French-Canadian voyageurs of an earlier time, first opening up the canoe country's vast water routes for the fur trade. As evening approached we headed our canoes to a point of land and set up camp in the leafless birch and spired spruce that fringed the shore.

The air remained balmy and still as a flaming sun slipped below the horizon. A hush descended on the land and none of us dared to break the spell. The quiet enveloped us and we steeped not only our senses but our entire selves in the blanketing stillness. The great wilderness silences seemed complete.

Suddenly the quiet shattered. Loons burst out with wild, rollicking calls of the intensity that only early spring seems to induce. Two yodeled crazily to each other, joined by a third, then yet another. Soon the whole lake seemed filled with loon laughter and excited tremolo calls. For me, more than any other sound, those enchanting calls epitomize these north woods. I knew at last, with a feeling that struck deep within me as the last call finally echoed into silence, that we had indeed reached the wilderness.

The next morning dawned clear and still. The lake lay like glass, so smooth that the shoreline of an island merged deceptively with its mirrored reflection. We lounged after breakfast, enjoying the beauty and luxuriating in the warmth.

That evening we camped on a many-armed lake, at a campsite facing west into the setting sun. The cool evening calm settled over us after the sun set. We soon spotted Venus, a brilliant diamond high in the western sky, as the spring peepers began their chorus. A male ruffed grouse drummed from across the nearby river, his muffled beating accelerating to a blurred whir. The sound of another river emptying into a lake far to the south reached us easily through the stillness. Only these quiet natural sounds reached us, merely adding to the vast solitude of a land empty of humankind.

I felt tranquil and peaceful that night. The all-pervasive calm of wilderness made us attuned and alive in that wild land. Already, after only two days in the wilds, we had cast aside our deadlines and schedules and picked up the simplicity of life in the wilds. Life in the canoe country seemed natural and right to me at that moment.

After breaking camp the following morning, we left the lake and paddled upstream toward the mouth of Barto Creek. All along our route we flushed mergansers and goldeneyes busy and excited with their nesting activities. Painted turtles basked on sunny logs. As we pulled the empty canoes up through a shallow riffle, dozens of large fish darted among the rocks at our feet. They, too, had felt the ancient urgings of spring, and now pushed upstream to their spawning locations. After a wild scramble, Dan caught one with his hands, and we discovered that we had chased a school of suckers. He let it go and we pushed on to Barto Creek.

At last we gained the mouth of the creek and began paddling upstream. Few people ever travel this region of swamp and alder brush. The area remains wild, and most people consider it unnavigable by canoe but for the high waters of early spring. With mounting excitement, we plunged ahead into this isolated region.

At the first rapids we found a glaring contradiction to the wild character of the land—the remains of an old cable-bound logging bridge built to cross this gorge several decades ago. Those logs and cable reminded me of all the battles waged over the canoe country the past century, early conservationists fighting dams, roads, airplanes, mining, logging, motorized travel—attacks against the canoe country that, if unchallenged, would have incrementally but cumulatively and irrevocably destroyed its wild character long ago.

We pushed on up the creek. We paddled broad, marshy valleys, then found ourselves facing narrow, rapids-filled ravines. After forcing our way through the brush and trees skirting the rapids, we would break out again to the swampy muskeg, tamarack, and black spruce bogs. We repeated this pattern again and again as the day wore on. Beaver dams and flooded waterways aided our passage and provided some stretches of paddleable stream. When the water depth dropped to impassable shallows, we unloaded and portaged along the marshy stream edges.

We made progress slowly at best. Sunset came and we quickly lost daylight, with our planned lake destination nowhere in sight. The creek curved back and forth so many times that we had lost track of exactly how far on the map we had come. We were weary and sore and wet. All this was part of the wilderness and, though we wondered how far we were from Barto Lake, we had had an exciting day. We decided to set up camp along the creek near a freshly built beaver dam and wait for good light in the morning.

Despite the uncertainty of our location and of the next day's travel, a sense of quiet delight crept over me as I sat there on the bank. We had seen the beauty of this fresh land in the last few days. We had sensed the vast wilderness silences, had thrilled with the wild calls of the loon. The canoe country sparkled with springtime excitement, and we had felt that excitement in the whitewater of the rapids. We now camped at an unknown location in unfamiliar country, but did not worry since we knew this special land and had the creek and stars as our guide. We had experienced significant physical exertion in our travels, similar to what wilderness author Mardy Murie had once written about the Arctic wilderness, "It is also the personal well-being purchased by striving—by lifting and setting down your legs, over and over, through the muskeg, up the slopes, gaining the summit . . . This wondrous mingling of weariness and triumph and sudden harmony . . ."

Tomorrow we would find our missing lake and crash overland, bushwhacking through the woods back to the "civilized" wilderness of portages and campsites. But the sense of wholeness we felt tonight would last long beyond tomorrow—this spring we had opened our siren wilderness with a fitting adventure and had become part of the canoe country at its finest time.

5

Wind-borne

I had canoed in many winds before, some gentle and balmy, others fierce and unrelenting. One day I had bobbed like a cork on huge, gentle swells so deep that at times I lost sight of my companions' canoes. Another time I fought the wind with breakers crashing over the bow of my suddenly tiny and frail canoe. Yet another time I raced for shore in a stiff crosswind while lightning chased me from behind. But this wind today blew differently from all others I had known, had a character all its own, one I will always recall with most vivid memories.

We had finished our trail lunch on the lakeshore, taken a swim to cool us from the bright August sun, loaded our three canoes with packs and gear, and pushed out into the lake. Ahead of us stretched a long expanse of water, seven unbroken miles to the east in one of the magnificent lakes typical of the Quetico-Superior canoe country.

I had noticed the wind that morning, but our travel then had crossed smaller lakes where it had no open reaches to unleash its strength. But as we put in at the far western tip of this lake, gazing at the hazy blue distances before us, I knew this force would soon be felt.

At first, as we paddled close to the protecting shore, the breeze seemed light and barely noticeable, easing our paddling efforts slightly. As we settled into a rhythm, I explored the sights of this lake I had never before visited.

The northern shore rose up from the lake, climbing steeply but evenly until it touched the cloudless blue sky at its ridgetop 350 feet above the water. The retreat of the last glacier some 10,000 years ago had carved out the lakebed and northern ridge, leaving bare rock and rubble in its wake. The entire expanse now wore a verdant blanket of many-hued green from the aspen, birch, spruce, and pine. The lushness of the forest came from the soil built up over the centuries, soil so thin that it measures in meager inches at its greatest depth.

I turned my attention to the southern shore. The tree species appeared identical to that of the opposite ridge, the lighter greens of the aspen and birch mingling with the darker conifers. But what caught my eye and focused my attention was the topography. Instead of the gradual, even ridge rising from water's edge, here stood plunging escarpments, rugged knobs, and cliffs. On this shore, as with many ridges in this locale, the sculpturing glaciers encountered harder rock, molten igneous rock that had solidified eons ago in masses resistant to erosion. Even the immense weight and gouging teeth of the great ice masses had not ground down this stone, leaving the impressively rugged landscape I now admired.

We had paddled several miles along the lake, with the wind gradually increasing in force all the while. Now our canoes sailed before the wind, making paddling a delight and canoeing a joy. The wind had churned the water to waves, our canoes dancing before the whitecaps.

But farther on we felt the full force of the gale. The whitecaps had by this time transformed into long lines of foaming breakers. Now we paddled with an exhilarating mixture of delight and caution, delight from feeling the power of wind and water, and caution and unease from knowing what that power could do. Our attention was riveted on paddling, balance, and riding the waves. Not risking a backward look, we judged the breakers by feel as they caught our canoe, then lifted, and finally thrust it ahead to settle us down between the swells. One error in judgment could send water washing over the gunwales, capsizing the craft far from land. And we could expect little help from the other canoes. Each canoe flew on its own now, each one separated from the others and fending for itself in the hissing combers.

Despite the threatening implications, the sound of those waves enchanted me. The breaking waves gurgled, foamed, and roared around us. The water had a voice of its own, one moment gently lulling, the next minute unnerving me with its thunder. Never had I canoed in sound like this before. I felt both excited and a bit fearful.

As we approached the eastern third of the lake, we began edging toward the northern shore, gradually easing toward a campsite nestled along the shoreline. The wild waters limited canoe maneuvers for us, but gradually all three canoes slipped closer to land, turning slightly toward shore in the troughs between the boiling crests.

At last we neared the campsite, where a flat shelf of rock angled down into the water between boulders and rocks. Here we required all our skill, for a false move could crash our canoes against the rocks. If we hesitated too long, the waves might force us past the campsite, with little chance of turning into the wind and paddling back.

We timed the waves and then, one at a time, darted for shore. The first canoe shot in, and the second one deftly followed to the rock shelf. As soon as a bow about touched shore, the crew bolted into the churning water and quickly pulled the boat from the waves. At last we all had landed safely, and we stood again on solid ground, a bit breathless from the excitement, relieved and exhilarated to have successfully made it to shore.

As the others explored the site, I stayed close to the water's edge. I gazed out across the waves and spray, not wanting to leave and break the spell. We had raced before the wind and skipped across those frothing whitecaps. I had become part of that powerful wilderness spectacle, part of the awesome force.

Our trip would traverse well over a hundred miles along the historic lakes, rapids, and portages of the Voyageur's Highway, where once the hardy French-Canadian voyageurs traveled the continent for the fur trade. We would know waterfalls, beautiful moonlit nights at cliff-top, spuming rapids, bountiful blueberries, and rain and mist on distant island-studded lakes. But today would retain a special charm for me above all the rest, and never will I forget this delightful sunny day, wind-borne down that long blue expanse.

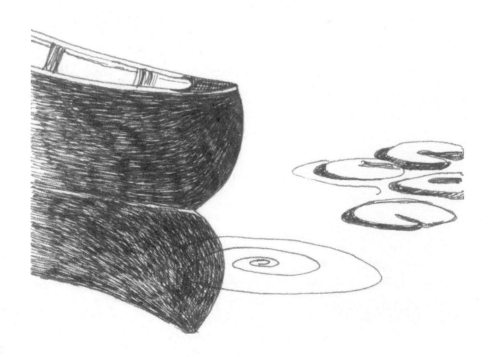

6

Caribou and the Whitetail

We decided to take a layover day today, to take it easy, swim, fish, and explore more of the beautiful lake in the Boundary Waters upon whose shores we camped. The winds blew strongly—the product, I suspect, of a high-pressure cell moving through. Canoe travel in these winds would be difficult at best, another reason to enjoy a layover day.

Jean and I paddled north of our campsite to a small bay hidden from the main part of the lake, sheltered from the strong winds. While stopped on a rocky shelf we saw a whitetail deer emerge from the woods farther down the shoreline and enter the water. We kept to our silence, and the wind blew from the doe toward us, so we quietly watched the deer while it remained oblivious to us.

Deer are not as common in the canoe country these days as they once were. Virtually unknown here during the pre-logging era at the turn of the twentieth century, deer invaded the area following the logger. The young aspen growth that emerged after the big pine had been cut or after the slash fires had opened broad expanses of the forest provided ideal browsing for deer. Their populations skyrocketed, even in the parts of the canoe country that escaped the axe and saw.

Deer carry with them a brainworm parasite, *P. tenuis*. While not harmful to the deer, the parasite is lethal to woodland caribou and can kill moose as well. With the invasion of whitetails, moose and caribou populations declined dramatically, caribou to the point where they completely died out from the canoe country by the 1920s and from all of Minnesota by the 1940s. Using the biologist's term, the woodland caribou became "extirpated" from Minnesota.

With abundant deer as a prey base, the wolf population also increased. Fortunately for the wolf, the caribou decline that resulted from the deer upswing did not mean a total loss of food for the canids. The wolves survived—and their population increased—as they switched their diet from caribou to deer, while continuing to catch moose when they could.

But now many portions of the forests of the canoe country have matured. Logging has ended forever in the Boundary Waters Wilderness, and areas like the Basswood Lake country, cut over from the big pine logging, have now reforested and gradually matured to conifers. While these restored forests provide habitat for other species, browsing materials are now scarce for deer in many parts of the canoe country.

But the forest has in some ways over-matured. Fire suppression over the decades has diminished the natural role of fire in the ecosystem, a role of regeneration and renewal, of restarting the process of forest succession. Without fire, natural openings and periodic disturbances have been eliminated and the forests may be even less hospitable for deer now than in pre-logging, pre-fire-suppression times.

But this maturation of the forest has also made habitat suitable once more for caribou, and declining deer numbers have reduced the incidence of *P. tenuis* in the wilderness. Biologists and conservationists have studied these changing ecological dynamics for many years with an eye toward restoring caribou to the canoe country someday, and a woodland caribou reintroduction project may yet occur. Attempts have been made elsewhere across North America to reintroduce woodland caribou to parts of their former range, some efforts successful, others not. Learning from these attempts will help any future Minnesota reintroduction project.

Common throughout the remainder of Minnesota, whitetail deer are almost over-abundant in some parts of the state, making it difficult for caribou to survive long in most places. The only location in the state that holds any realistic chance at restoring woodland caribou is the Boundary Waters, with its right mix of coniferous habitat, boreal forest, and low presence of deer. Even with the recent blowdown in the area, and the warming climate that would seem to favor deer over caribou, the exciting prospect of restoring this missing element of the ecosystem fuels the hopes and dreams of many conservationists, biologists, and wilderness visitors.

Wilderness areas across the nation provide habitat for threatened and endangered species. Largely undisturbed by humans, wilderness areas have offered refuge for these rare species where they have become extirpated elsewhere. The magnificent California condor, for example, with its nine-foot wingspan, was rescued from the brink of extinction through conservation work and captive breeding efforts in zoos. The condor has now been restored to the wild in wilderness areas in California and Arizona, far from the disturbances and impacts from people. Other imperiled species need the same refuge in wilderness.

Prior to the protections of the Endangered Species Act, the canoe country itself offered the last refuge and reservoir for the eastern timber wolf in Minnesota. With the protections of this law and from this stronghold, the wolf has since recolonized much of northern Minnesota where it once thrived. The Quetico-Superior could yet play a similar role in the restoration of the woodland caribou to its historic role in this ecosystem, making the area ecologically whole once more.

The tawny whitetail doe at the water's edge drank calmly from the lake, alert to her surroundings but still unaware of our presence. Eventually she ambled back into the woods. Though exciting to witness this wary, vibrant animal in the wild, I look forward to the day when we might thrill instead to the sight of—or just knowing about—a woodland caribou returned to its native canoe country in the Quetico-Superior.

7

Broad-wing

Broad-winged hawks are often seen or heard soaring above the woods and forests of the Quetico-Superior canoe country. These medium-sized *buteos* (from the genus of broad-winged soaring hawks) inhabit thick woods like these, hunting for food in silent stands of pines, spruce, or aspen, or floating over openings in their search for food. Smaller than their *buteo* cousins, the red-tailed hawks that also live in the northwoods, broad-wings have a body length of about sixteen inches and a wingspan of about thirty-four inches.

Yesterday as we paddled the sheltered and hidden bay of the lake on which we camped, Jean and I witnessed an amazingly close view of a broad-wing. We had paddled the shoreline, exploring the nooks and crannies, the rock faces and the granite shelves that gently sloped to the water's edge.

We both caught a glimpse of something falling from a tree—a large piece of dead bark floating down, I first thought, so irregular was its movement. But suddenly we realized it was a bird.

The broad-wing plummeted into the bush at shore, pouncing no doubt on a mouse or vole or other tasty morsel. The hawk did not see us until it had landed, so intent had it been on its dive. Then it realized we were there and took off flapping rapidly just in front of our bow, then switched quickly to a soar. We had marvelous close looks at it, the dark edge along the trailing edges of its wings, the black-and-white striped tail, its curving beak. What a great sight!

The broad-winged hawk is fairly common throughout the eastern United States and southern Canada. Both males and females have the same plumage though, like many hawks, females are often larger and heavier than the males. Nesting pairs spend much of their time beneath the forest canopy, hunting for small animals. They catch and eat mostly small mammals, but they will also capture amphibians, reptiles, insects, and small birds to bring to their nest.

Fortunately, broad-wings remain quite numerous throughout their range. They are one of the most abundant hawks in North America, and one of the most abundant *buteos*. They did not seem to suffer population declines during the era of DDT as did other raptors like the peregrine falcon.

In the fall, broad-winged hawks migrate to Central and South America, where they spend the winters. The hawk we saw yesterday is a long-distance migrant, traveling from the U.S.-Canada border of the Quetico-Superior thousands of miles south to Mexico or South America.

During its fall migrations, this bird will begin its southward journey from the Boundary Waters to the north shore of Lake Superior. There it will fly southeastward to the western tip of Lake Superior at the city of Duluth. There it may join other broad-wings in large flocks or "kettles" that may include hundreds or thousands of birds that soar and swirl together past Hawk Ridge before heading further south on their flight. Tens of thousands of broad-winged hawks are sighted each fall at this point, the most numerous of any of the raptors counted there.

Today, on our last portage of the day, I noticed some splattered guano on the bushes and shrubs along the trail. With the canoe overhead, I could not see much. After finishing the portage I returned along the trail, my vision now unobscured by the canoe. About twenty-five to thirty feet up in a mature aspen, I spotted a stick nest nestled in a crotch at the trunk. As I moved to a better vantage spot, I saw a downy young hawk staring over the edge of the nest and down at me. There may have been others in the nest, though I couldn't see them. Broad-wings often have two or three eggs in each clutch. An adult broad-wing soared and called high above, perhaps the same hawk that dove near our canoe. I thought I'd better not disturb them any longer, and I turned around on the trail to join Jean.

This hawk of the deep woods also nests there, rather than near shorelines like bald eagles and ospreys—hidden and protected in the forest itself. Always exciting to see, the broad-wing hawk remains an emblematic symbol of the deep forests of the canoe country.

8

Arctic Cold

We snowshoed down the trail and out onto South Hegman Lake on a brilliant winter day. We came prepared for winter camping and the cold, even if we had already had one false start.

Yesterday we came in to Mule Lake on a trail that had been snowshoed once already this winter and had been recently cleared of most deadfalls. Our travel, therefore, came pretty easily and we made good time. We had camped overnight in the snow and the fairly mild winter temperatures after packing down the snow with our snowshoes to build a tent pad.

Earlier today we rejoined the trail that skirts around Mule Lake heading to the north. We followed it with ease, thinking we would make Stuart Lake easily by lunch.

But the trail remained good only to the first windfall complex. There the trail, as well as the faint snowshoe track, disappeared. We floundered around a mass of downed trees, blown over perhaps in the windstorms of last summer. The deep snows and downhill terrain make our progress excruciatingly slow, all while carrying our heavy fifty-pound packs. Snowshoe tips were buried in deep powder on occasion, and I eventually tipped over into the snow. Floundering with the pack on my back, I eventually righted myself with the help of my ski poles. Finally we snaked our way through the blowdown to clear terrain.

But now where was the trail? With deep snows, no blazes or markers on the trees, and no track to follow, we proceeded by educated guess and the look of the land. We did eventually find an old sawn log, and knew we were on the right track. We continued on until the next deadfall tangle.

Here we were perplexed; the trail had disappeared. We checked the map, stepped over some deadfalls and deep snows, angled up a steep slope and dropped back down. Still we were perplexed. But soon I picked up a faint snowshoe track and on we headed, climbing up a hill heading east, then turning north again to snowshoe through a nice jack pine forest.

But soon we came to the worst deadfall tangle so far, with no clues as to where the trail went. We guessed and angled up to the left after traversing deep snows and deadfalls, all precarious maneuvers with our packs. We were rewarded with a sawn log. But where next? We angled upward to the left, toward the high point of land. We finally made it to the top of the hill, my left snowshoe binding loose.

I was exhausted at this point, straining to catch my breath, my back and shoulders aching from the heavy pack. Dave's knee had begun to hurt. More than a little uncertainty about continuing this course had crept into my mind. We stopped for a break and looked at the map. This trip had become much more difficult than expected.

Reluctantly, we decided to backtrack to Mule Lake, rather than flounder through innumerable windfalls and wonder where the trail ran. We could struggle in this fashion all the way to Stuart for all we knew, even if we could find and follow the trail. At Mule Lake, we could follow Mule Creek to Stuart, and at least be certain where we were.

So we backtracked. Near the black spruce swamp, we left our packed trail and crashed on toward the lake. Deep, sinking snows and a few deadfalls slowed us even here. We floundered on until we reached the lake.

Again we looked at our situation, the half-day or more we had already spent, and decided we didn't want to camp in the Mule Creek swamps that night. Instead, we decided to backtrack farther to the Echo Trail and head to South Hegman Lake. We could spend a couple nights camping there, explore the lakes, see the pictographs, and watch for wildlife. So we did.

All the way back out to the Echo Trail, again on the packed trail, we noticed the snow sculptures, the red and jack pines, sunlight playing on the snow, a well-broken path ahead of us, knowing where we were and where we were heading, and glad we made this decision. We would enjoy the winter wilderness yet, even if the Stuart Trail had foiled us.

We camped at a site on South Hegman that night and spent the next day leisurely exploring around and trying to stay warm. The temperature had dropped overnight, to probably ten or fifteen below zero Fahrenheit, so we took longer getting going in the morning than the day before.

Our boots had frozen stiff overnight, and both of us had to bring them into our sleeping bags to loosen them enough to wedge our feet inside. Everything had frozen. We slowly got up, had a late breakfast, and then went exploring for the day—without those heavy packs. We snowshoed up to North Hegman and up to the pictographs. Not a cloud touched the sky, and our day was filled with bright sun, lots of white snow, and rocks. It was a beautifully sublime day, as Dave and I liked to say.

Someone had taken the mile-and-a-half trail north from Trease Lake to Angleworm, leaving it nicely packed. We followed the trail for half the distance through the gorgeous winter woods, then turned around and headed home to camp. Still we had seen no other people.

The temperature dropped with the sun; we could be heading for twenty below or colder during the night. Dave and I finished supper, made preparations for bed, and headed for the tent. Inside, I discovered that my boots had frozen on my feet so solidly that I couldn't get one of them off. Though I hadn't stepped in water, the perspiration from my feet and the bitter temperatures had frozen the boot quite solidly. Only with Dave's assistance did I finally force the frozen boot off my foot. Then I tried to thaw the boots and felt liners inside my sleeping bags. The temperature became so cold that my pen froze as I tried to write in my journal once I slid inside my bags. I had to blow on it constantly to warm the ink.

The temperature plunged overnight, far lower than even twenty below. We would learn later that the temperature plummeted to about forty-three degrees below zero. Despite the extreme temperature, the fog clouds in our tent, and the hanging ice and frost crystals everywhere, Dave and I stayed warm enough through the night. We each had two sleeping bags, one inside the other, and we slept somewhat comfortably through the Arctic night. We were slow to move in the morning, though, and the sun had been up for a couple hours already before I first ventured out of my bags. We were both reluctant to leave their warmth.

It was cold.

Despite keeping my boots in between my sleeping bags overnight, frost still covered the insides and the soles were still frozen. I was able to stuff my boot liners inside my inner bag, though, and work my feet inside them relatively easily, unlike the night before. At least they were pliable. Once on my feet again, though, the boots refroze.

I checked my little thermometer after I stumbled out of my bags; it had already warmed up to twenty-seven below. I stomped my feet and ran laps out on the ice to keep moving while Dave got up and dressed.

We decided to punt on breakfast and just head out. We quickly dismantled our frigid camp, packed up, strapped on the snowshoes, and headed out over the surface of South Hegman. My feet—which had been at their coldest of the entire trip—gradually warmed under the exertions of snowshoeing with my heavy pack.

The sun shone brightly again under the influence of our Arctic high pressure. The still morning was absolutely quiet but for a fluffed-up gray jay that visited our camp and a raven croaking overhead. Glad that we were not stuck deep in the wilderness dealing with the challenges of this frigid weather, we snowshoed up the trail, leaving behind our winter wilderness and the Arctic cold.

9

Denizen of the Depths

We were paddling the shores, sliding along through the grays of an all-day rain in mid-September in the canoe country. We had covered over a dozen miles since the morning, had fought stiff winds and whitecaps, taken shelter from the storm and waited out its worst, and paddled in downpours. We had stopped once to ward off the early stages of hypothermia by heating and guzzling hot drinks. Now, near the end of our long day's journey and more than a little damp, we glided along another shoreline, the gray hues of rain and clouds and distance merging and surrounding us.

But along this shoreline, we spotted something in the needles and branches of a recently fallen spruce. At first glance it seemed to be a large dark green-and-brown garbage bag that had escaped an earlier camper, now caught by the branches and trembling in the breeze.

Then we realized it was alive, that it was not a garbage bag but a huge snapping turtle. We quickly turned the canoe to investigate closer, hurrying before it disappeared into the water.

As we drifted in, however, the turtle did not move or slip back into the water. It was the largest snapper I had ever seen, about two and a half feet across the top shell, or carapace, from head to tail. The center of its carapace had a dished look to it, too, since the shell had grown so large that a good five or six inches now spread between what are normally the mid-ridges of the carapace. The carapace was so large that it appeared to have a certain amount of flex to it, not the rigid hard shells of the smaller snappers I was used to seeing. This turtle was huge!

Now we were almost on top of the animal and it still had not moved. It had not even seemed to notice us, yet we had glided in so close that BT or Ed could have touched it with their paddles. What was keeping it there? Was it tangled somehow in the branches? Was it even still alive?

The common snapping turtle (*Chelhydra serpentina serpentina*) lives throughout southern Canada and much of the eastern United States, including the Canadian Shield country and the lakes and rivers of the Quetico-Superior Ecosystem. The turtles eat about anything they can catch, including fish, frogs, crayfish, and even young birds or young waterfowl. Though fast swimmers, they prefer to hunt slowly or motionless, then strike their prey with an eye-blurring jab. Their powerful jaws and long, strong neck make the snapper a formidable predator. The official state record for the largest snapping turtle in Minnesota, we learned later, is just under twenty inches across the carapace, much smaller than the one before us.

At last the giant noticed us and looked up, seemingly annoyed by our intrusion. It was not tangled or caught, as I had thought, but slid quickly into the dark waters of the lake. Only then did we realize the full story.

A second turtle, almost equally as large, had lain underneath the first. It, too, quickly slipped into the dark waters of the lake and disappeared from our sight. The turtles had been intent on each other, not us. We had interrupted them, these monsters of the deep with their surprisingly flexible and shiny green carapaces. With them, we had had a glimpse of something ancient, something primeval.

The turtles were an exciting reminder to us of the diversity of life found in the Quetico-Superior wilderness. This richness—the complexity of all the natural biological life found here, from lichens to ancient red pines, from microscopic invertebrates to turtles to moose—is often referred to by ecologists as biological diversity, or biodiversity. The rich variety of the region, and the interactions and interplay of all the area's biological life, represent some of the primary ecological benefits that come from protecting wilderness areas.

Often only wilderness areas or large parks contain the full array of species, this full richness of nature's bounty. Other areas that are more impacted or developed by humans have often lost species and become more biologically impoverished as the degree of development or impact has increased. Elsewhere, the biggest predator of the snapping turtle is man. People often hunt or kill snappers, sometimes for their meat, and sometimes simply because of our fear of this seemingly ugly primordial-appearing reptile and its powerful jaws.

Yet these turtles—like all species—have their own special role in the ecosystem, irrespective of our human-oriented, anthropocentric views of their appearance or our fears of these powerful predators, or regardless of whether we even know or appreciate their role and function in the natural world. Living in the protected wilderness where human predation is extremely low or altogether absent may account for our snappers' enormous sizes and corresponding ages. These turtles may well have been over thirty years old.

We left the spot of the turtle rendezvous and turned our canoe once more into the enveloping grayness, our dampness and cold temporarily forgotten. As we paddled off, we marveled still at the turtles and our encounter with these denizens of the depths and the rich biological wealth they represent here in the canoe country wilderness.

10

The Encounter

The fireweed bloomed now only from the very top of its flowering stalk, and the goldenrod and large-leaf aster also displayed their blooms. These were some of the signs that it was late August, the end of another summer season in the canoe country wilderness of northern Minnesota.

We had come for a brief visit to the beautiful Boundary Waters, all four of us, to give the girls another experience here, another taste of this special wilderness that was once again threatened. But on this trip I was also hoping to see the wilderness through the girls' eyes, or at least try to, and share this glimpse of the canoe country with them.

We entered the wilderness through an old-growth forest of red and white pine. Bud Heinselman, our friend and famed forest ecologist, had loved this stand, had studied it, and had fought to protect it as wilderness. It had originated from a fire in 1822, Bud had discovered, so the tall trees towered over us, their trunks rising straight to the skies. Just earlier this season, the Forest Service had conducted a prescribed fire in this stand, to restore this agent of change and disturbance to the ecosystem. The fire was intended to open the forest floor to sunlight, much as fires had historically done in stands like these for centuries before the advent of fire suppression. The fire appeared to have done its job, eliminating balsams, shrubs and other understory trees that could have provided ladder fuels for a crown fire in the tops of the pines. The tall pines appeared undamaged by the prescribed fire for the most part. Bud would have been pleased.

We put in at the foot of the portage and began our leisurely paddle along the shoreline. The familiarity of the canoe country came rushing back over me, as I gazed and smelled and listened. I fell comfortably back into the role of guide, explaining massive bedrock on the shore and its lack of soil, how the trees cling to cracks in the bedrock slabs where soil has built up. A gray jay fluttered from tree to tree on the right. A soaring turkey vulture floated overhead, seemingly unstable on the thermals.

We swung the canoe into an out-of-the-way bay, Maja sitting on the bottom of the canoe between Jean's knees in the bow, Carlye on the bottom just ahead of me. I had brought my pole and a spinner, and Carlye was enjoying her first experience of trolling as we paddled. We began a slow arc around the bay, first past a campsite, then past the lake's outlet, a tiny stream flowing out between slabs of bedrock, eventually to tumble into a lake below outside the wilderness. We paddled on, taking a break to fill our water bottles with cool, clear wilderness water to pass around with a snack. We passed a second campsite and then turned toward the mouth of the bay where we had entered.

Suddenly a splash broke the water's surface behind us. I turned to look. "Carlye, do you have a fish?" I asked.

"I think so!" she replied excitedly.

"Set the hook and start reeling in!" I called. Her six-year-old's excitement could not be contained as she reeled in. A second splash.

"I have a fish!" she shouted. There came yet a third splash as the fish broke the surface of the water once more. Carlye's strong arms and hands had brought the fish, still unseen by me, close to the canoe, where it dove deep into the depths. But eventually she brought it up to the surface again. All four of us shared her excitement, tinged, perhaps, by our species' deep-seated impulse to catch one's food from the wild.

Finally the fish rose to the surface, tired for the moment. I lifted it up. A beautiful smallmouth bass, two, maybe two and a half pounds. Carlye promptly named her Annie. Carlye wanted to release her, so after a couple of photos, we set her free, with hopes that we might see Annie again in a few years. We paddled to the portage and a lunch break, replete with the gurgle of the nearby stream as well as wintergreen appetizers.

Though the afternoon would be filled with many other special moments, from floating alongside ancient pictographs to gliding past pitcher plants and sundews in a bog, the encounter yet to come overshadowed not only these, but the exciting rendezvous with the bass as well.

The girls traded places in the canoe after lunch. Maja, the big three-year-old, sat with me trying to match her big sister's fishing exploits. Carlye sat just behind Jean and ahead of Maja. Maja would eventually hook a wily bass of her own, but one that would tangle the line on an underwater snag.

A large cloud had covered the sun, providing welcome relief from the glare and heat. Off to the right, Maja and I spotted a pair of loons, playing and chasing each other. One was rearing way out of the water. Then we spotted something else there swimming. A loon chick? We turned and glided soundlessly, all of us quiet, straining to see the mystery.

The mystery turned out to be not a family of otters, as I next had thought, but a seemingly common sight—a family of beavers. Two adults and a kit swam and splashed as we glided closer. One adult came swimming directly to us, checking us out, snorting as it neared. We all sat as still as stones. The adult swam closer, still on the surface, looking us over. It came to within five or six feet of the bow, unafraid but curious. The other adult and kit swam around, unalarmed by our quiet presence.

The curious adult swam around and came back near us, again to within a paddle's length of Jean in the bow. The girls practically quivered with excitement, but remained quiet and still.

The three beavers continued to swim around, occasionally diving and resurfacing, still not concerned with our seventeen-foot canoe floating in their midst. By this time we had spotted a beaver lodge along the shore nearby, the likely home of this castor canadensis family.

The curious adult came close a third time. This time, however, it saw or sensed something of concern. It lifted its tail, dove and, in the same motion, slapped its tail in a resounding ker-thump. The other two beavers quickly vanished from sight at the sound of the warning splash.

We sat there another moment in quiet, enthralled by our close encounter with the beaver family. Then the girls began talking excitedly about the beavers and how they swam out to greet us, and the loud splash it had made. Jean and I had enjoyed the encounter as well, and were pleased with the girls' excited reactions.

Though our silence had certainly aided the encounter, this family of beavers had likely never heard an outboard, never been jarred by the noise of an engine. They had not learned to fear people in the wilderness, seeing only an occasional canoeing party pass through their lake.

Even if our close encounter was with the common beaver, the same animal that had brought the fur trade of the voyageurs here centuries before, it nevertheless was filled with the solitude and silence, the mystery and wonder born of wilderness, nurtured in wilderness, preserved in wilderness. It was a close encounter we would long remember.

11

The Portage

Wilderness areas offer challenges—and joys—through traveling by primitive means. In the ice-free months in the Quetico-Superior canoe country, this usually means by canoe and portage trail. Wilderness travel often also means encountering the unexpected and learning to deal with wilderness on its own terms. A trip from early in my guiding career taught me this lesson.

The adventure had started out on the right foot. We had begun the day before, Marty and I and a group of high schoolers, from Isabella Lake in the southern portion of the Boundary Waters Canoe Area Wilderness. Neither of us had ever guided in this area before, and a sense of exploration and discovery enveloped us as we paddled down the Isabella River to the west.

We surprised a good deal of wildlife along the river that sunny day. Mergansers and goldeneyes flushed ahead of our canoes, and great blue herons rose ponderously at our approach. A bald eagle soared over one stretch of the river, and we startled four moose at various spots feeding in the shallows. This stretch of wilderness seemed a wildlife paradise.

We camped that night on Bald Eagle Lake, a sprawling lake three miles long with a dozen or so campsites nestled along its shores. In the morning we began heading northeast, leaving the watershed of the Isabella for that of the Kawishiwi. The lakes sparkled brightly but the portages were long and tiring as we climbed and descended the intervening ridges.

After one particularly long portage we found ourselves in a small pond, connected to the main body of the lake by a meandering stream. The water level in it had dropped, however, due perhaps to the washout of a beaver dam ahead. At any rate we attempted to paddle the swampy stream, but soon found paddling impossible. Only an inch or two of water lay atop the muck and mud.

Despite our situation, the area held its own special beauty. Pitcher plants thrived here, their hollow, water-filled leaves used to trap and dissolve insects. Another insectivorous plant, the sundew, grew atop protruding stumps near our canoes and resembled miniature Venus flytraps. Blue flag, the native blue iris, enjoyed the acidity of humus and soil on the occasional hummocks.

We struggled to make progress with the canoes. I hoped to stand on whatever footholds available to pull the lightened canoe ahead toward the lake beyond. The method worked to a point, but at times I sank to my waist in the mud before feeling a submerged log on which to stand. Smelly methane gas from the decomposing organic matter in the deep muck emerged from my floundering steps. The others fared even worse than I, and progress came tortuously slow. And the lake still lay far out of sight.

We had to try something else. I slogged over to the right on trembling mounds of floating muskeg to the nearest group of trees. These black spruce trees thrived in swampy habitat like this, and this stand grew thick and dense. I searched for a portage trail not marked on my map, but I had no such luck.

While wandering among the close-growing trees, though, I stumbled across a faint animal trail, a deer run perhaps, that wound among the trees. I followed it, losing it now and again but hoping against hope that it ran in the direction of the lake. The path climbed upward and topped out far above my companions. The thick spruce cast cool shade all about, and a thick cushion of moss, ground pine, and bunchberry grew beside the barely discernible trail. Then I saw the blue glint of an open lake farther on below me.

If we could only follow this faint trail and squeeze packs and canoes between the trees, we would soon cruise open water again.

Upon my return I relayed this good news to our swamp-weary crew, and we began our "portage" crashing through the woods. Tricky footing and the faintness of the trail hindered our progress; the canoes, however, caused the greatest difficulties. Maneuvering in thick woods with seventeen-foot canoes overhead involved seemingly endless backing up and forward thrusting to clear the canoe's ends for even slight turns of the trail. At places the canoe gunwales stuck tightly between close trees, and I quickly learned the art of carrying a tilted canoe on one shoulder to squeeze through. Shoulders aching and with mud-encrusted boots from the swamp, at last we broke free of the clutching spruce and paddled once more on open waters.

Years later I passed along that route again, vividly remembering that day with a perspective gained from far more experience in the canoe country and unhampered by the immediacy of the original situation. This time we had the same low water level, but the swamp looked not nearly so formidable nor did our plight seem quite so desperate. I recalled the trials of that first day to my companions and pointed out where I had first entered the thick spruce woods.

As we neared that spot, I was surprised to notice signs of human traffic at that place even though, as before, the map marked no portage trail there. But as we carried our packs and canoe up and through the spruce, I saw now a regular trail following almost exactly the animal trail I had first followed years before. The passage of many travelers since had widened and packed the trail to distinctness. Some of the clutching branches had been cut, and the trail now bypassed some of the worst-obstructing trees and the tightest canoe-wedging spots. Other than such minor changes. the trail and its route remained much the same as before. Once again, we soon paddled on open water.

As we pushed out again into the welcome open lake, I felt the years roll backward. In pioneering our little portage trail we had seen the birth of all portages in the canoe country, from obscure trails like ours to historic trails like the Grand Portage itself. All such trails had started like this one, all had widened and become more distinct with each party that came behind. We were akin to all portage-blazers of the past and had left our own trail for other voyageurs to follow. And in doing so, we had vividly experienced the struggles and joys of wilderness travel on our own portage trail.

12

Late Winter Thunder

Ireturned to the canoe country for a final time this winter, to snowshoe through the woods and over the ridges, to be alone in this wild land.

Two feet of snow still filled the woods, the buds of trees and shrubs still dormant and waiting for at least another month's warmth and sunshine. But by late winter the temperatures usually moderate, and traveling the BWCAW at this time of year typically avoids the hassle of contending with twenty or thirty below.

I came from several hundred miles to the south, and as I drove north to the Canadian border I stepped backward from early spring to late winter. Snow was absent as I began the drive, but as I continued northward the snow reappeared, first as small patches in shade, then as lingering drifts, until finally the ground was completely white again.

The weather, however, surprised me. Air temperatures soared to the mid-fifties in the canoe country as if the early spring I left far to the south had leapt after me to challenge the deep snows of winter in the silent woods.

I unpacked my car at the trailhead, dressed in short sleeves in the warm sun. I readied my pack and strapped on the snowshoes, swung the pack to my back, and headed north.

The snows lay thick yet, but the sun and warm temperatures had done their work. I sank with each step in the wet, heavy snow, always at least four inches, and sometimes up to a foot. The snow had melted and loosened enough that in places it collapsed at the touch of my snowshoe, chunks of snow sinking a couple of feet around each snowshoe. In places huge plates of snow collapsed up to twenty feet ahead of my steps.

Travel under such conditions was arduous. I slogged along the unbroken trail, sinking with each step and catching loads of heavy snow atop each snowshoe. Every step became a chore, as it felt like I lifted forty pounds of wet snow with each foot. Progress came quite slowly.

Then, as I neared a small, frozen bog, thunder ripped the air. A thunderstorm sent angry gray storm clouds toward me from the northwest. Again thunder rumbled. A late winter thunderstorm!

Nearing sunset anyway, I hurriedly looked for a spot to camp. I snowshoed toward the bog's edge, found an open spot with a view across the bog to the cliff and pines on the far side, and began to pitch camp.

I stamped down an area for the tent with my snowshoes, packing the snow for a tent pad. I took off the snowshoes and hurriedly pitched the tent, sinking occasionally through the packed snow with my boot. Thunder cracked overhead and lightning flashed

around me. I shook my head in wonder at such unusual weather while winter camping in the snow.

I threw my gear inside the tent and followed it in myself. I sat by the door, removing my boots as the rain finally hit. Suddenly high winds buffeted my tent; lightning and thunder ruled the skies overhead. I anchored the tent with snowshoes driven deep into the packed snow as the winds threatened to blow my tent away.

The storm blasted overhead as my tent shook in the gale. Rain continued to fall for some time. The lightning and thunder eventually moved off to the southeast. As the woods quieted and the sun reappered, a saw-whet owl called to the north with its almost mechanical, beeping call.

In all my travels in the canoe country, this weather certainly ranked among the most bizarre. It was symbolic, perhaps, of the uneasy transition from late winter to early spring, as spring attempts to shoulder aside a winter reluctant to depart. Soon winter would relinquish its grip for good and spring would arrive in full force here in the wilderness.

After supper, the sky darkened and the clouds moved off to the east. Orion slid above the horizon low in the southwestern sky, closely followed by Sirius. The constellation Bootes had just climbed above the eastern horizon, while Leo the Lion dominated the southern sky. The Dippers circumnavigated the north, as usual.

I stood watching the sky just outside my tent. Though I had sweated and trudged through the wet heavy snow, lugged a cumbersome pack, fell awkwardly at times in the deep snow, and hurriedly made camp in the face of an unexpected storm, I felt contented and at peace, familiar with the land and comfortable with my usual wilderness routine. Again I had reduced life to simple terms here. The spot I called home that night was remote and wild, and possessed a charm its own, enveloped by the natural silences of an enchanting land that captivates me so.

The breeze sifted through the jack pines overhead. All traces of the dramatic late winter thunder had disappeared.

13

Vistas

Wilderness travelers often revel in the vistas they encounter on their adventures. Whether it's a panoramic sweep of wild country from a mountain peak, or the long reach down a wilderness lake, these vistas add meaning and delight to a trip.

Today I stood before such a wilderness vista, this one in the Quetico-Superior canoe country. I had climbed high above a lake on a rugged cliff named Thunder Point. Here I looked westward down the length of Knife Lake, a large, long lake down whose middle runs the international border.

As I watched from the heights I spied a tiny canoe paddling into the westerly wind. I could have just as easily been watching a scene from 200 years ago, when the birchbark trade canoes of the French voyageurs paddled this very lake, paddles flashing in the sun and their *chansons*, or French songs, echoing along the shore. Here, too, they gazed at the distances ahead, as they did so many times on their 2,000-mile fur trade route between Grand Portage on Lake Superior and interior posts like Fort Chipewyan on Lake Athabasca.

This view was a particularly satisfying one for me. Two islands were anchored side by side in Knife, guarding the confluence of the main part of Knife and the equal South Arm. The green forests, with all their variances in shade across the rugged, glacially formed topography, covered the slopes and ridges as far as my eyes could see. No development, no buildings, no power lines marred the view; it was the same as it had been for two hundred years or longer.

But perhaps most important of all was the open horizon far to the west near the Isle of Pines, toward which I would paddle when continuing my journey. It was this view and these horizons that influenced me today, and these vistas with hazy blue distances that have influenced much of my life. They speak of wide stretches of wild country, of adventure and exploration and mystery, of places that have escaped the domination of human civilization. They tell of echoing loon calls down the sweep of a wild lake, and of the howling winds that sometimes blow down them. All these things and more add their richness to a wilderness vista. Wilderness travelers know the meaning of such long wilderness vistas and they always enrich trips in the wilds.

I remember one wild vista in the High Arctic on Canada's Victoria Island. Slowed by high winds and cold temperatures, we remained wind-bound one evening. We climbed up on a promontory that evening in the midnight sun, looking ahead over the tundra at the course our river took in and out of lakes on its tumble to the Arctic Ocean. We matched our maps to the vista below us, saw the route before us, and returned to our campsite ready for our travels ahead.

On another trip in the High Sierra country of California, I spent an exhilarating night high above Yosemite Valley. The full moon bathed the peaks of the Sierra Nevada Mountains with its light. So enchanting was the scene that I could hardly sleep that night as I roamed around, gazing at the panoramas of glistening moonlit granite peaks all around me.

Humankind has always had a great need for wild vistas and open horizons, one with a basis in evolution itself. We must gaze at distances and dream, whether that is to cross a continent by covered wagon or fly to the moon. Against these distances and these unknowns, we continually test ourselves, gauge our progress, or simply gaze and dream dreams.

The wilderness traveler intuitively and intimately knows these things. Whether it is the vastness of a deep canyon, the distant snow-clad mountain peaks, or the panorama from on top, such travelers seek out these vantage points and their views. This impulse is as old as our race itself, this desire to see beyond oneself. It may have begun as a defense measure to protect primitive people from animals or marauders, or as the desire to gain a vantage point to seek out a route, plan an attack, or to search for shelter or food. Whatever the origin, this desire is so deeply ingrained in us, so much a part of our pool of consciousness, that even today in our mechanized, nuclear age this search continues, although for perhaps different reasons than before.

Wilderness areas like the Quetico-Superior preserve these unchanged vistas for decades and even centuries. Though the individual trees may change, or the forest cover itself may change over the span of a century, a wilderness area preserves its vistas from development or harm so future generations may know the same views as previous visitors, to test themselves in much the same way as those who passed through before, to revisit their ancestral past. The vista from Thunder Point really has remained essentially the same, thankfully, since the voyageurs paddled through this same lake, strengthening my affinity with those hardy paddlers of a bygone era.

I slowly climbed down from the heights of Thunder Point and returned to my canoe. I shoved off, pointed the canoe west, and began paddling down that wilderness waterway I had enjoyed from above.

14

Winter Renewal

I stood still in the woods, with soft snowflakes falling gently from the sky to melt upon my cheek. Only the occasional crow call broke the muffled silence of the winter woods. It was deep winter in the Boundary Waters.

I had come in the day before with my companions. Slush on the lakes had made skiing nearly impossible. We had opted instead for snowshoes, far better anyway than skis for travel in the thick forests of the canoe country.

A bright sun shone brilliantly yesterday on the thick mantle of sparkling snow, and the clear January sky arched vividly blue over the land. We began snowshoeing from a large lake normally the companion of summer canoeists; now the lake knew silence and snow.

We broke a trail from the lake across a frozen marsh, through brush and woods and over a ridge before eventually arriving at a small hidden lake. Here few people traveled; the long route through the thick woods kept most summertime paddlers to larger lakes and well-trod portage trails.

Though the country seemed frozen and quiet, we saw evidence of life etched on the snow's surface. A bounding fox had crossed an open stretch of snow-covered ice, dragging its claws slightly along the snow's surface. An otter had smoothed out its slide along the shore of an island where it had scampered and slid down again and again. A pine marten had left its seemingly oversized hind prints on a snow-laden bough.

After our lunch break on the small lake, we snowshoed over a ridge, through another marsh, climbed a substantial hill and dropped down through quiet woods to another small, remote lake. Here we selected a sheltered site and set up camp for the evening. The silent cedars near shore would block most winds, and the fallen trees farther in provided fuel for supper's fire.

The night remained fairly warm—just above zero—and we enjoyed a fairly balmy evening. The sky darkened quickly while we finished supper; suddenly sharp, bright stars filled the night sky. Orion and Sirius dominated the eastern sky, while the Hunter and his Dogs chased Taurus the Bull across the winter sky. A few traces of the aurora danced along the northern horizon.

I left my companions after breakfast the next morning. They went one way, I another. I traveled quickly at first, moving at a brisk pace to warm up. Soon I slowed to a more leisurely pace, stopping to absorb the sights and sounds and moods. I paused for a moment and knelt to tighten a snowshoe binding.

This time alone was the most special of all. I traveled by myself and enjoyed the solitude. Small things delighted me: the sight of perfect wind-swept snow shapes, the stark simplicity of a red osier dogwood stem against the snow, the snow-topped curl of birchbark peeling from a truck. I came to more fully appreciate the creak of my snowshoes, the crunch of snow underfoot, and the encompassing silence.

Snow began to gently fall, softening the outlines of the tall red pines atop the nearest ridge. The sun shone dully behind the layers of clouds and falling snow, not able to penetrate the skies this morning. A lone chickadee called once from the nearest shore.

Now, as I stood alone listening to the silence on this soft gray morning, I felt invigorated, excited, and refreshed. More quiet adventures waited ahead and I was renewed by the winter experience here in the wilds. It's not too different, I thought, than what winter does for the wilderness itself. Both the wilderness and I have to go through dormant times of renewal and recharging before the exuberant burst of spring.

Life had not left the land, as we had seen, but awaited the end to the cold and snow. Those animals that had not migrated south either continued their activity with winter adaptations or slept the winter away. Plants and trees in the canoe country relied on the period of winter dormancy, patiently waiting for the coming warmth and life's return. Winter was the time for winnowing and survival and renewal.

Finally I broke my reverie and pushed on, past a leafless birch into a thick stand of green, snow-covered spruce. I snowshoed up the hill through the silences of the thick winter woods. Soon I broke through to sunshine.

15

In Search of Remoteness

BT and I had returned to the canoe country in September, seeking a way to bushwhack into one of the most remote regions of the entire Boundary Waters Wilderness. Though all the BWCAW is a designated wilderness, the remote tract we sought was truly wild wilderness, with no portages, hiking trails, or designated campsites. In addition, we had been warned that this area was a tangle of blowdown trees, impossible to traverse. We expected a physically grueling trip, but one well worth the effort for the satisfaction of visiting truly remote tracts of wilderness, where few if any sane travelers visit.

And in this expectation we were not disappointed.

BT and I had made many such crashing trips off the beaten track in the quarter-century since we began guiding wilderness canoe trips together in the Boundary Waters and Quetico. We loved these trips and reveled in the physical challenges as well as the rewards they brought. It was, in fact, on one of our earlier trips several years before where, huddled in the tent one cold and rainy night, we identified this isolated area on the maps. That started us wondering how best to work our way into the area, visit its small lakes, and bushwhack our way back out again.

And finally we were back.

We spent much of the day making our way to this small, remote lake, on whose shores we now sat at dusk. From the "civilized" wilderness of portage trails and campsites, we had portaged overland to a small stream, bushwhacking through the under-growth and trees while carrying our packs and the canoe. The stream, though narrow and meandering, offered enough water so we could paddle most of the way to the first of the distant lakes we sought. This pretty lake had high cliffs and ridges along the southerly shore. A short stretch of paddling brought us to the second lake, equally appealing.

From this lake, we planned to paddle another stream, but here the travel became more difficult, foreshadowing the grueling work

ahead. Stretches of the stream we could paddle, but occasionally it disappeared into piles of rocks, with steep ridges on both sides. Here we disembarked and stumbled up the ridges through thick forest and blown-over trees, burdened with packs and canoe. At one such carry through the woods, we found ourselves atop a steep ridge with no easy way back down to the water. BT slid down ahead, and I carefully lowered the packs and canoe down to him before we could begin paddling again, only having to repeat such carries—again and again.

Near sunset, after a final bushwhack through the woods, the stream opened up to another lake. A bald eagle flew from its perch near the mouth of the stream. A good omen? Tired and scratched up from our travels, we decided to spend the night here.

We wearily set up camp, enjoying this remote lake, wondering whether anyone had ever camped here before. This little gem was our home for the night, in some of the most inaccessible country we'd ever visited in the Boundary Waters. The solitude, the great silence of the wilderness, was all-enveloping. The rewards of traveling to this remote spot were immense, no doubt enhanced by the physical difficulties in reaching it.

Despite the satisfactions of the evening, still I had a feeling of apprehension, an uncertainty of the unknown. Would we safely make it out? Would the travel and bushwhacking be as tough or tougher tomorrow as they had been today? Would the stream on which we hoped to paddle have enough water in it this late in the fall? This uneasiness I sensed, this apprehension, are also part of the wilderness experience. Canoe trips on regular routes are now often predictable and routine, and lack this increased sense of the unknown. Our heightened sense of awareness, attuned to the wilderness around us, came in part from our remote and isolated location, deep in the heart of the wilderness.

Solitude—the sense of isolation, being out of touch with modern society—is one of the great intangible characteristics, and rewards, of a wilderness experience. Solitude encompasses silence and quiet, and a lack of contact with others. But there is more to solitude than just those attributes. Solitude includes an isolation from civilization, its technologies, its schedules, its communications. It is also a state of mind, where one's response to the environment is unaffected by the artifacts of civilization.

True solitude is increasingly hard to find in our ever-shrinking world, made all the smaller by increasingly sophisticated communications technology. Wilderness areas offer some of the few places where one can truly feel isolated from the frenzy and rush of society, where one can explore uninhabited country away from others. Many of us need these places to provide the solace and balm needed in our modern society, to provide opportunities to immerse ourselves in wild nature, to evoke a sense of humility, and to inspire reflection and awareness that we often lose in our bustling world.

BT and I sat at the edge of this tiny lake, crouched on a small shelf of somewhat crumbling gabbro bedrock. An owl, completely silent, flew to us in the dark, barely visible as a silhouette against the lingering light in the western sky. We could discern no markings in the dark, but it was about the size of a barred owl. It flew over us, circled behind, and perched in a tree. I tried a barred owl call ("hoo-hoo-hu-hooo, hoo-hoo-hu-hoo-ah") and it instantly took flight, coming back to pass silently over us again. Again I called, and for a third time it returned and soared on silent wings right above us, so low that had we stood up, we could have touched it. Then, as quietly as it had come, it flew off into the night to return no more.

Another omen? In some cultures, such an encounter would certainly have held meaning, and not necessarily a good one. For us at that moment, however, we knew no hidden meanings in this encounter, and it would be days yet before we could attribute any other meaning in it.

Meanwhile, this magical encounter on our search for remoteness made all the toil worthwhile and infused us with great excitement and thrill. Tomorrow we would meet the great challenges as we worked our way through miles of backcountry travel and grueling work to get back out to the wilderness of regular travel routes. But for tonight, the rewards of this remote wild spot had already more than made up for them.

16

The Scramble

We had returned to the Quetico-Superior country, hiking into a special area of rivers and waterfalls. We first took a short detour along the west side of a large river to see a precipitous falls, which I had not seen before. We climbed about halfway down to gain a view of an even more spectacular falls. It was a grand sight, and we paused for some time, not wanting to rush from this hidden scene. But then we climbed back up and onto the trail again, headed for a campsite along a much smaller stream.

We hiked to the campsite and ate lunch. Our daughter Carlye had not been feeling great, but had willingly come along for the hike. We spied the gorge into which the stream cuts and dives and then disappears. Then we decided to hike down to see the waterfall from the bottom. It was not a short or easy descent, and we needed to make a wide arc in order to work our way to the base of the little waterfall.

It was a steep scramble, half sliding down the steep terrain to reach the stream below. We clung to trees, branches, and rocks to keep from tumbling straight down. The kids, of course, made it down first. Once we arrived, we followed the stream bed back upstream toward the falls, through brush and brambles, up and over boulders and logs. At last we all reached the falls, where the stream falls into a little cavern, where quartz chunks lay scattered about, and where the air temperature was considerably cooler. It was a fun and exciting scramble, and everyone had made it there safely.

Getting back up was another challenge. We found a slightly less steep spot to begin working our way up. Again it was quite a scramble, often on all fours as we climbed up out of the gorge, higher and higher. Finally we reached the campsite once again.

After we began hiking back on the trail back out, Carlye told me that she was finally feeling great. She was tired from the clamber down and back up, of course. Her legs were scratched and bleeding, with one knee scraped from all the scrambling, but she had loved the descent to the falls and back up. "I have a good time when I get banged up and scratched," explained our rough-and-tumble soccer player. There is a lot of wisdom in her observation.

I believe this is one of the truths about wilderness travel, too. By hiking or canoeing under one's own power, the experience is more personal, more rewarding, more vital, more real. Expending energy and our physical exertion makes a wilderness experience quite real in a way that simply being flown in to the same spot could never do. In the process, we often get banged and scraped and scratched, and it often puts us, like Carlye, in a much better frame of mind. We interact more personally and more intensely with the wilderness around us when we travel this way, and our experiences remain vivid to us for long afterwards, perhaps from the magic of earning the them in this way.

Others have recognized this as well. Harvey Broome, one of the founders of the Wilderness Society, marveled while watching his friend, Ernest C. Oberholtzer, portaging his ninety-pound, forty-year-old wood-and-canvas canoe. Ober, then seventy-two, had spent decades exploring and fighting to preserve the Quetico-Superior wilderness. Broome wrote,

> Ober knew also—deeply within himself—of the need for great physical activity, for the juncture of body and mind and soul in a unity of effort. He knew the rewards of paddling and the primal delights of the portages. Physical effort, the slow timing of a world gauged on physical

exertion, the peace to the soul and body which went with these, could still be found up here in the beauty that was left.

Sigurd Olson wrote of this once, about flying into a favorite lake deep within the Boundary Waters in the years before it was illegal to do so. He felt the same way about not working his way into the heart of the canoe country by the paddling and portaging he normally did, by not earning his way into the wilderness. Though his favorite campsite looked the same and he caught several lake trout there, his whole experience was less meaningful to him.

"I knew, however, what I must do the next time," Sig concluded. "I must go in with pack and canoe and work for the peace of mind which I knew could be found there. I would be a mole again and learn the feel of rocks under my feet, breathe the scent of balsam and spruce under the sun, feel the wetness of spray and muskeg, be part of the wilderness itself."

I had a similar experience once on a canoe trip to the Bloodvein River, which arises along the Ontario and Manitoba border and flows westward to Lake Winnipeg. My canoeing partner Braden and I had planned to drive to the end of the road and paddle several days to reach Artery Lake, the headwaters of the Bloodvein. But at the last minute we combined our trip with another group of friends, and we ended up flying into Artery Lake instead of working our way through the wilderness to get there. Artery Lake looked beautiful once our floatplane had dropped us off, but the experience was not nearly as meaningful to me as if we had spent several hard days of paddling and portaging to reach it.

Such physical encounters with nature are one of the benefits of a wilderness experience. In our hectic, fast-paced civilized world, with modern work-saving appliances and vehicles, travel in wilderness areas forces us to reconnect with our past, when many people worked outdoors and experienced a connection with nature through the physical exertion needed in wilderness travel. Physical activity helps us appreciate more deeply the wilderness through which we travel, and triggers a deep response within us that heightens our awareness and reflection. Our scramble down to the small waterfall with Carlye helped me remember this great benefit of wilderness.

17

Deep in the Heart of Quetico

I had canoed to the center of Quetico on a long solo trip. I came for the solitude, the kind that is sensed most keenly when on a solo trip in the wilds, far removed from people and the signs of civilization. I had also come for the adventure, for the freedom of traveling through wilderness country on one's own, and for the intense awareness and attunement with the natural world that wilderness journeys can often bring. I found these and more, deep in the heart of Quetico.

An immense satisfaction comes on a trip alone like this. Days out in the backcountry, I knew that I came all these miles under my own power. I could look at my gear and know it was everything I had here in the wilderness, all that I had to rely upon. The sense of freedom and independence was almost unparalleled; I went where I wanted and when I wanted, and had to rely on my own strength and resources to see me through. I could stop to climb cliffs or sit in the sun, or I could paddle all day and make camp at sunset.

I had already paddled many miles on this trip, had experienced fine travel and found a rare plant found nowhere else in Quetico. I had also encountered rain and winds, with big waves and wind that spun my lightly loaded canoe around in an instant when I wasn't careful.

One day I did indeed climb a cliff. The day was perfect, and I sat atop the huge cliff at the south end of my lake, which stretched out below me to the north. This was the view I had longed for, and this vista alone made the entire trip worthwhile. The climb to the top had been long and very difficult in places with no trail to follow, but the panorama below me made every step and every risk worthwhile. It was a great prelude for the day ahead.

There are days when canoeing is difficult and paddling burdensome. Clouds of mosquitoes on portages, wallowing in mud, or falling with the canoe atop your shoulders make trips a challenge. Fighting wind, waves, or weather can make a trip by canoe in the wilds something to be endured, not enjoyed.

Not so today.

The breeze blew gently from the south, and I headed north along a long narrow chain of lakes, the breeze at my back. Paddling today was ecstatic—I had slipped so completely into the ancient rhythm of wilderness living that my strokes were effortless, thoughtless. I glided north along the shores, conscious only of the beauty around me. The feel of the paddle in my hand felt so right, the movement of the canoe like the wind itself. I was so euphoric that I found myself laughing out loud for the joy of it all. In all my years of canoeing the wilds, I had never felt such joy, known such contentment from the paddling of a canoe. This sense of wholeness and oneness, of excitement and exploration is what I sought on this canoe trip, and it came flooding over me with the breeze from the south.

At one point, I drifted alongside ancient Indian pictographs painted on a cliff. I could discern the images of three moose, a canoe, faded hand prints, and other indistinct markings.

Later, as I floated northward, soundlessly absorbed by my surroundings, a large adult black bear began swimming the southern channel of the lake, crossing right in front of me. So soundless was I that the bear did not seem to even notice me or my canoe. It swam swiftly across, and then emerged on the western shore.

I slipped northward, miles sliding by. I stopped for lunch at the water's edge, completely absorbed by the wilderness spectacle around me. I could hardly divert my attention to lunch, so compelling was the attunement I felt. I didn't want to miss an instant. After lunch I headed still north, still completely captured by the lakes and woods through which I traveled.

All too quickly I finished my northward sweep and found myself at last on the large lake on which I planned to camp. I had reached the most northern point of my route there and began winding my way through the labyrinthine channels of the lake. Just at that point I spotted a cow moose and calf swimming across the channel in front of me, large ears flapping frequently, alert to my presence. They reached the point on the shore before I did, but I

did have some close looks at them along the shore before they disappeared into the woods.

The breeze that helped blow me northward earlier was now in my face as I turned southeastward. Paddling came much slower now. As I cruised behind a small island—hugging the shore due to the wind—I spotted a loon on its nest. It laid low, its head on the ground, as if to hide from me. Suddenly it scrambled awkwardly to the water and proceeded to dance, call, dive, and surface. At times it approached to within a few feet of my canoe, when it would abruptly change direction and call its excited tremolo, hoping, I think, to lure me away. I obliged, wanting to move off as soon as I could so it could return to its nest.

Finally I reached the south end of the large island along which I paddled, and headed for a much smaller island in the channel, with a rocky wind-swept point in the breeze. No bugs there tonight. Later, just past sunset, the high wispy cirrus clouds—mare's tails—were still blowing over. The moon was about one night before first quarter. After twenty-eight miles of travel today, I would sleep soundly.

Deep in the heart of Quetico, enveloped by the great solitude and silences of this wilderness, I felt so alive, so attuned to the world around me. Solitude is certainly much more than being alone. For me, it is also a frame of mind and the mental freedom that come to me in wilderness, disconnected from the outside world. Some feel that privacy and isolation are elements of solitude, but I have also found this attunement and oneness on wilderness trips with others. Because it is enhanced by an absence of other distractions, like motorboats, mechanized devices, unnatural noise, or crowds of people, solitude on wilderness trips facilitates a self-discovery and awareness of a person's deepest needs and feelings and spiritual connections.

My friend and mentor, Sigurd Olson, also experienced this solitude on many of his trips in the Quetico-Superior. He wrote once,

> I have traveled as my friend did many times, and while I love to have companions with me, I discovered long ago what psychologists call 'creative silence': the impact of solitude on the mind, the awakening of ideas and thoughts normally hidden when one is with others, the emergence of concepts often lost owing to interruptions and responsibilities. During such times, one drinks from the deep wells of the past.

This solitude, this oneness, also encompassed the kind of awareness and freedom I experienced on this day of wilderness travel, apart from the sights and sounds and smells of civilization with its noise and motorized trappings, instead focused so completely on the wilds around me. I had experienced much this day in the heart of Quetico, and it in turn had given me something profound in my own heart.

18

The Exploration of Unnamed Creek

My seven-year-old daughter Maja and I had come to the north country in May, a beautiful time to be in the woods. We had come backpacking with two friends along a river that flows between the Boundary Waters and the North Shore of Lake Superior. The woods were alive and vibrant with the excitement of spring, and we felt this exhilaration as we set up our camp within earshot of the roar of a rapids.

The river was like so many others in this part of the world, meandering in the level places, sluicing down exposed bedrock in rapids and small falls, and slicing its way through gorges as it worked its way resolutely downward toward Lake Superior.

Twice after making camp, Maja and I went exploring up a small side stream that flowed into this river. The stream had no name. Streams like this, if marked at all on maps by the state, often receive the unimaginative title of "Unnamed Creek." It was not large, and not much water flowed through it. It had no outstanding geological or biological features, but it was wild and unknown to us.

It was great fun to explore with Maja. "Dad, it's so exciting. This is the best time I've ever had outside!" she told me. We boulder-hopped back and forth and then back again up this stream. Maja led the way, so excited and animated, choosing the route, hopping from rock to rock, then from bank to bank, under alders and over logs. We went past yellow marsh marigolds still in bloom, a lavender violet, bluebells, and vivid white patches of wood anemone. An ovenbird sang out its call through the woods. Farther and farther we pushed upstream, Maja intently pressed on exploring the unknown. What lies around the next bend? Where does this stream come from? Do small fish swim in this deep pool? Would a moose come here to browse? What might we discover? On and on we explored up this wild stream, away from all signs of people, alone in the woods.

The mystery of the unknown, the excitement of exploration and discovery, is one of the true deeper values of wilderness and wild country. My friend Roger Kaye has shown this in his research on wilderness values of the Arctic National Wildlife Refuge in Alaska. He found that the aura of mystery and the urge to explore it is one of the important meanings of wilderness, and that the aura of the unknown deepens the wilderness experience.

I have this same appreciation for discovery and exploration of the unknown from my many wilderness trips in the canoe country and elsewhere. On many of my canoe trips in the Boundary Waters and Quetico, I have relished exploring places off the beaten track, places where portage trails are not marked on maps and few people ever venture. These journeys have always been rewarding, as I bushwhacked or portaged or paddled to places few others would ever think of exploring. The thrill of adventure and excitement as we pushed to these unknown spots made all the extra physical work well worthwhile.

I remember one Arctic canoe trip in a remote corner of the Northwest Territories of Canada. We hiked and explored unnamed canyons and places far from the river we traveled. We had seen a falcon aerie high atop one cliff, where the peregrines that swooped overhead that day had earlier nested. The excitement of exploration had filled us then, as we thought—or imagined—we may have been the first people, at least the first non-native people, to visit those hidden places.

This exploration and discovery are simply not there, if this were tame country, developed and well-defined by humankind.

There are lovely natural places in the Twin Cities, for example, including the Mississippi River Gorge not far from our house. But appealing as they are, they lack the essence of mystery and the unknown that makes exploration in wild country so alive and vivid, compelling and rewarding. Had Maja and I hiked along the inviting but tamed Minnehaha Creek in Minneapolis, for example, we would have had a nice time, but not the excitement of exploration of wild and unknown country with no other humans around.

Maja and I hopped on farther, crossing this beautiful, unnamed stream again and again. We clambered over fallen tree trunks and swung under overhanging branches, with her leading the way. At one point, Maja's foot slipped as she jumped across the stream, soaking her shoe. But that didn't faze her. The excitement and intrigue of exploring the unknown lured us on and on. It was hard to stop.

Finally, however, we stopped to catch our breath. We decided to finally turn around and wend our way back to camp and our friends. Such fulfilling exhilaration and excitement had been ours, for we had explored this wild natural stream during the special rush of spring. Though not spectacular scenery or remote and rugged terrain, our creek had nevertheless energized and excited us far more than a dozen tame views of even a spectacular Grand Canyon or Yosemite vista from the road. We would remember our nameless stream, and our exploration of it, for a long, long time to come.

19

Images of Autumn

Dave and I returned one autumn for our year's final paddle through the border lakes. Neither he nor I had ever before begun a trip at the obscure entry point we chose, so it was the excitement of exploring new territory as well as the anticipation of a week in the October wilds that buoyed our spirits as we shoved off.

The heavy rains earlier that fall had left water levels high for this time of year; water lapped shorelines normally high and dry by October. The stream we began paddling seemed full to the banks, and we had plenty of water to paddle our way along the winding channel. Three low-level beaver dams temporarily obstructed our passage along the tamarack-lined route, but these we negotiated handily and slid the canoe over with ease.

The route we took for this trip was the historic border route, well-known from the days of early white exploration of this country and the route of the subsequent fur trade of the French voyageurs. Our trip would traverse much of the length of Ontario's LaVerendrye Provincial Park, established to protect this international border route. We planned to end our trip with the nine-mile Grand Portage from the Pigeon River down to Lake Superior, carrying our canoe and packs over the long trail to the reconstructed fort on Superior's shore.

We entered the area that day at an entry point that gave quick and easy access to country along the international border. While fast and convenient for the two of us that trip, the easy accessibility provided by our entry point and others like it has also diminished the remoteness of this historic wilderness route.

Remoteness is an intangible quality, an essence, but a key component of the wilderness experience. Remoteness carries with it a sense of isolation, the chance for solitude, a heightened awareness. Crowds of people can diminish remoteness; while one can travel in an isolated wilderness setting, the sense of remoteness can still be impaired if surrounded by too many people.

Remoteness is obliterated by roads and access points. Too many entry points in any wilderness create easier accessibility, resulting in formerly remote routes or areas being quickly penetrated. When that happens, something about the wilderness has changed for those who visit there. The sense of isolation and remoteness is lessened, and the land's magic is cheapened by the new ease and increased numbers of people who reach it.

Old-timers like Bill Rom told me that years ago the Isabella River-Parent River route offered a terrific, remote two-week canoe trip, returning via the Kawishiwi River country. But over the years, the Forest Service allowed a number of "accidental accesses" to be built along the southern edge of that route, mostly to facilitate logging when it was still allowed in the Boundary Waters. Now there

are official wilderness entry points all along that route, from Little Gabbro Lake on the west to Kawishiwi Lake on the east. The remoteness of that old canoe route is now greatly diminished by the easy access of the half-dozen or more new entry points.

On our trip this autumn we would see no other canoe on the border route waterway, despite the presence of cabins on some lakes not within the wilderness. Late October, we discovered, is a perfect time for solitude here. After a harried summer of tens of thousands of wilderness paddlers, the land now appeared empty of human visitors.

Solitude and remoteness can still be found in the canoe country even in the summer, but they are increasingly hard to find. New roads, easy access, and too many entry points diminish remoteness and solitude in both the BWCA Wilderness and LaVerendrye Park.

Remoteness and solitude—these things fortunately surrounded us on this late October trip. No disturbance from other people, no shouts from loud groups, no racing other parties to the last open campsite. Even most summer resident birds had migrated and had left this land by now. We had seen only some ravens, gulls, and a few late loons.

A few weeks earlier the country had blazed with the colors of autumn. The birches reached their golden peak first, followed quickly by the bright yellows of aspen stands. Maples added their special touch of fire on slopes and shores.

But the colors of the landscape through which we paddled were muted now, the subtler hues of late autumn. The deciduous trees and shrubs had shed their leaves weeks earlier. The ridges on which these trees stood looked bare and empty, the white trunks of aspen and birch in large stands completely exposed by the fallen leaves.

Even the tamaracks had lost their tawny gold needles, and only a trace of their ragged tarnished gold remained along the banks of creeks or marsh edges. The ambers and tans of grasses and sedges lined the washed-out blue of reflected sky and clouds.

This time of late autumn is one of expectation and waiting—expectation at the uncertainty of the weather and a waiting for the ultimate first hard freezes and early snows.

We canoed across gray, wind-swept lakes, the entire country to ourselves. We carried our gear over wet portage trails, through quiet forests whose floors were sprinkled with brightly fallen leaves. The dark green shores of balsam, spruce, and pine were lightened by the stands of bare birch, and brightened occasionally with a rare patch of golden yellow not yet fallen.

We delighted in the solitude that was ours. We paddled on across large lakes, underneath towering cliffs, and through small, still ponds. We headed on toward the Pigeon River and Grand Portage, with thoughts of remoteness and accessibility amid these vivid images of late autumn.

20

Timelessness

On my first solo canoe trip in early May in the Quetico-Superior many years ago, I experienced a sensation of freedom and release that I had not known during the previous half-dozen summers of guiding canoe trips there. Not tied to the needs of a group nor confined by the daily schedules of camp chores, meals, and travel when traveling with others in the wilds, I delighted in my newly found freedom.

I spent hours one morning tracking down fleeting glimpses of warblers, mostly Myrtle warblers and one black-throated green, bushwhacking to an unexplored small lake off my main line of travel, and paddling soundlessly down a creek in hopes of viewing birds and other wildlife. And I did it with a new sense of freedom, completely independent of another's time or fancy. The timelessness and the completely unhurried pace were some of my new discoveries on this trip.

That night it began lightly raining as I fell asleep; the weather was finally changing. The air temperature had dropped by morning, and when I awoke, the ground was covered with snow. I procrastinated in my warm sleeping bag—listening to the bird calls outside was my excuse. A ruffed grouse drummed, a kingfisher chattered along the shore, and other unidentified birds occasionally peeped. Later, I went out exploring the woods around my campsite through the snow and decided not to break camp, but to wait for the weather to break. I returned to the tent for a snooze.

Later that day I found that the heavy, snow-laden clouds had broken up and blue sky peeked through the clouds along with the sun. Basking in the sheltered, sunny shore, I had superb close looks at the many warblers flitting through the bushes: many Myrtles, an American redstart, a Nashville warbler, then a black-throated green, and finally a pine warbler. The snow had all but vanished in the sun and warmer air temperature.

That afternoon I went exploring. I paddled to the east of my campsite, checking out the shoreline. I found my flock of warblers had moved there from the campsite: the redstart, several Myrtles, several Nashvilles, and some chipping sparrows that I seemed to herd along the shore as I quietly paddled along. I bushwhacked up to a small lake nearby, checked out some campsites, and paddled to the base of some cliffs. The sky cleared off completely by late afternoon, so I expected to travel the next day.

After sunset and a quick supper, I watched the sky. The shading and hues from west to east struck me as quite beautiful. The reds and oranges, of course, are usually associated with sunsets and were found low on the western horizon. Then came a section of yellow, although not very wide or bright and often covered up by the brighter reds and oranges. At rare times a distinct green was visible, followed by bright blue that covered most of the sky. Toward the east, the blue faded to a rich deep purple, finally followed by the distinctly dark night sky. In the time following the sunset, each of these colors was visible and constantly changing as they followed the sun below the western horizon. Finally the dark purple-black of night gradually dominated the sky until, at last, the night had fully arrived.

That day had been remarkable. It had been touched by the little things, the simple things that wilderness life can bring. I watched a front blow over, dropping snow that I later watched vanish. I stole many delightful glimpses at the excited little warblers flitting in the woods. I leisurely explored a previously unknown (to me) lake. I delighted as I listened to three loons yodel crazily back and forth as they patrolled my bay, as only loons in the early spring can do. A barred owl also hooted out its "Who cooks for you, who cooks for you-all?" call from a nearby perch.

Perhaps best of all, I stood or sat completely still and quiet, sometimes ten or twenty minutes or a half-hour at a time throughout the day, all my senses straining to catch the meaning of it all. I could do this, and open myself to such awareness, because of the timelessness of wilderness.

Timelessness is one of the great rewards of wilderness travel. It allows us to break with the often overscheduled calendars of our normal lives, and provides freedom and opportunity for great awareness and receptivity. Though I have enjoyed this sense of timelessness on many wilderness trips with others, I often find it at its best on solo trips.

My day was not governed by the clock, by the schedules of a group, the urge to keep traveling despite the weather, or the regular times for meals. I never take a watch on any of my wilderness trips, leaving it at home so it cannot impose artificial schedules or deadlines on my days, and this trip was no exception. I allowed the timelessness of the wilderness to rule my day, and an immensely rewarding day it had been.

21

The Light Show

Last night our rocky point, and all the surrounding canoe country, witnessed a fabulous light show. A series of three fierce thunderstorms swept over our point, lighting up the skies with nearly continuous lightning.

The storms marched in from the northwest, blasting everything in their paths. The first storm held almost constant lightning, flashing like a strobe light, lighting up my tent so brightly that I didn't need my candle lantern or flashlight to see. Peal after peal of thunder ripped through the air, surrounding us on all sides. As this storm moved atop us, bright flashes of lightning made the night like day, followed by an almost instantaneous crash of thunder. Rains fell with this first storm, though not very heavily.

The second storm moved in on the heels of the first, the lightning not quite as intense, but impressive nonetheless. With the second storm came the winds. As it approached, a solid roar moved down Lac La Croix, almost like a train heading our way. Hail began to fall. I thought of straight-line winds—or perhaps a tornado—and I nervously perked up, watching and listening.

The lightning still flashed, and suddenly the winds hit our point, buffeting my tent and pummeling the area with hard, wind-driven rain. I listened for the canoes, hoping they wouldn't fly off. Rain drove into my tent door, which I reluctantly zipped up midway. Yet my tent held, despite the pounding, and I stayed fairly dry. Soon this second stormed passed over, and I dozed off once again.

The third storm soon arrived, less forceful than the others though it, too, brought lightning, winds, and rain. The third storm spent its fury on our point, and soon passed to the southeast. The rains continued to fall, and an occasional bolt of lightning still flashed, but the storms had moved off.

Our spectacular light show had ended. Three inches of rain had fallen.

Though I had not been frightened for my safety during the storms, I recognized that risk is—and should be—an inherent part of the wilderness experience. Land that is wild and untamed by humankind contains all sorts of risks to those who visit. The challenge of safely encountering and surmounting those risks adds to the delight of seeing and traveling through wild country.

This is not to say that I turn a callous heart to those few who are injured in the canoe country or, even more unfortunately, die on their visits to the wilderness. Sadly, fatalities in the Boundary Waters and Quetico do occur on an all-too-frequent basis. Drownings cause most deaths here, but others have died from heart attacks or freak accidents.

Some visitors have died from lightning strikes not unlike those I witnessed during the wave of storms on Lac La Croix. Lightning can strike people on the ground or out in a canoe on the water; sometimes a lightning bolt travels down a tall pine and through the tree's roots to reach someone camped on or next to the roots.

Several times during other canoe trips I have seen a paddling companion's hair begin to rise and stand on end as a thunderstorm approached, sending me the strong signal to move off the open water immediately. And move quickly I did! Fortunately I have escaped any serious consequences of lightning at those times, as well as on my rocky point during the light show.

Should wilderness ever be made risk-free? It could not and should not. Do I want to fall victim to accident or death in any wilderness? Of course not. In our litigious society, where we are often trained by legal liability exposure and insurance companies to minimize or eliminate liability and risk in wildlands, such notions of risk run counter to the prevailing norms. But wilderness areas must and should always retain that certain challenge, that element of risk for those who travel there. Part of the challenge for those of us who relish visits to wilderness areas is to accept that risk, know about the potential hazards of wilderness travel, think and act safely while in wilderness, and come prepared to meet the wilderness on its own terms.

The skies had cleared by morning after the light show on Lac La Croix. Though the ground was soggy and our equipment damp, blue skies and sunshine beckoned us on.

22

Awakenings at Dawn

The summer night was clean and calm. The stars shone brilliantly during the early night. Later, the waning gibbous moon arose, lighting up the night sky.

In the morning, at dawn, all was calm. The sky remained clear; no breeze disturbed the still air. The sun had not yet risen. Slowly, the sky brightened further. Far in the distance of Lac La Croix, a loon faintly called out. Here on the island, a nuthatch called in the pines. Other than these small sounds, the dawning morning remained calm, quiet, expectant.

In the half-light of dawn, the stars gradually faded as the sky barely, almost imperceptibly, began to lighten. The growing lightness of the sky overwhelmed the stars one by one. I enjoyed this time, not moving, but happily and intensely aware of the wilderness world around me slowly turning to light, slowly awakening to morning life. The hush surrounded us, overwhelmed us. The great wilderness silences remained complete.

Still later, the sun finally peaked over the eastern horizon. Yet all remained quiet and calm. No breeze touched the tops of the pines under which we camped. No one else was out of the tents yet. My companions, if awake, remained silent like me.

Then suddenly, seemingly from nowhere, the great lake awakened. Waves began lapping the granite shoreline, gently, easily, but still no breeze could be detected from my vantage point. It almost appeared that the lake itself had begun to breathe, waking with the morning. Perhaps some riffle, some gentle breath from the far reaches of the lake to the north had reached us.

It was a perfect start to a wonderful wilderness day.

Yet no voice had broken the silence, the quiet of dawn. My companions did not want to end the magic moment any more than Jean and I. One of our voices, the snap of a stick, even the crackle of a fire would break this quiet time and push us into the busyness of preparing breakfast, packing up, and paddling off on our day's journey. But for now, for a few more moments, all that could wait.

A nuthatch called once more, closer to us than before, its nasal call subdued.

We would later pack up in sunshine and warmth, a pleasant change from yesterday's winds and clouds. We would later take a long last look around our campsite, my old familiar site, one of my favorite spots in all of the canoe country, with its views across to Canada, situated along the old historic fur trade route. Later we would load the canoes, head south toward Boulder Bay and paddle on glass for miles.

But not quite yet.

Later seven-year-old Ella would joyfully find her special stick at the portage where she had forgotten it a few days earlier. Later we would paddle the length of Agnes Lake and camp on Nina-Moose Lake. Later ten-year-old Dean would finally catch his walleye and his Dad, Art, a fat smallmouth bass. A morning later we would exit our beloved wilderness, without the time to spend these moments of dawn in quiet, in listening, in expectation, in awareness.

All of that would come later. But for now, that perfect moment of dawn remained. Our senses were attuned to the new morning, our ears straining to catch every sound. The lake had awakened, the day had begun, the silences remained.

23

Wind and Fire

Our family returned to explore Seagull Lake, a large island-studded lake mostly within the borders of the Boundary Waters Canoe Area Wilderness near the end of the Gunflint Trail. A massive windstorm had swept across the wilderness recently, blowing down trees in a swath that stretched over several hundred thousand acres of the canoe country. Seagull Lake, we had heard, suffered extensive damage from the blowdown. I wanted to see for myself.

Carlye and I paddled one canoe, while Jean and Maja took the other. We paddled the old familiar route out into the lake from Wilderness Canoe Base where I once had guided—around Dominion Island, past the old Timberlane campsites, across the outlet of the lake that flows north to Saganaga Lake, and past the invisible wilderness boundary into the official Boundary Waters. Next we wended our way through the islands, past the Palisades, and around Miles Island to its northerly campsite we once called the Cupboard Campsite. Here we stopped for lunch. I had been looking closely for the signs of the blowdown. Up until we reached this campsite, I had not seen much evidence of it. Even the tall red and white pines on the east and north sides of Miles Island had survived the winds in pretty good shape.

But at the Cupboard Campsite, the blowdown had done its work. What once was a shady campsite of towering red and white pines 300-400 years old had been dramatically changed. The hundred-mile-per-hour winds from the "derecho" windstorm had raked across these tall pines on the exposed west end of the island. Most had snapped off or blown down. The power of the wind had done its work. Fallen trees and sunshine had replaced the shady grove of ancient pines I remembered and loved. The changes saddened me, to see my old familiar giants toppled all at once.

After lunch we continued on, paddling west down Seagull to the Alpine portage. Again, we didn't see much evidence of blowdown until we reached the portage. The once-familiar portage trail—previously shaded by tall jack pines—now ran through a fairly extensive area of open, sunny blowdown. Again, the incredible power of the storm could be seen, and it was an awesome spectacle to see nearly every tree of the canopy snapped off or blown over. Ecologists have speculated that the many decades of fire suppression in the Boundary Waters had resulted in an older forest than otherwise might have been here, making it more susceptible to the fierce winds.

Our campsite on Alpine Lake had also had some trees blown down, though certainly not all. We camped here, with lots of room for the girls to roam and explore. The loons still called on the lake, a bald eagle soared overhead, and the wind still rippled the surface of the lake while a white-throated sparrow called through the woods.

As awesome as the blowdown was, however, it certainly didn't destroy the wilderness. Changed it, yes, but not destroyed it. This wilderness ecosystem has adapted to these periodic disturbances, has evolved to survive them, and in fact needs disturbances like windstorms or fire to recycle nutrients and regenerate the forests. And the windstorm was, after all, a natural event, albeit one on a monumental scale. Though it was sad for me to see a favorite campsite like the one on Seagull so radically changed, it is only part of the same cycle of disturbance, renewal, and growth that has shaped the wilderness here for millennia. Though I miss those ancient pines, I know that the wilderness will survive and thrive past this particular storm.

One of the very reasons we set aside and protect wilderness areas is to allow these ecological and evolutionary processes to operate as freely as possible from human intervention. Forest fires, windstorms, disturbance, and succession should be able to function in wilderness areas without the manipulations we often subject those forces to elsewhere. Such processes are as vital to the ecological health of the wilderness as the biological components—the trees, wildlife, plants, and so forth—that we more frequently notice.

We need to remind ourselves of the need for patience and humility when it comes to wilderness. Our species desperately needs patience, because wilderness areas operate on time scales well beyond our own human lifetimes. The forests of the Boundary Waters need lots of time to produce a stand of 400-year-old red pines, well beyond the reach of a single human lifetime. And humility, to remind ourselves that wildernesses need to operate on their own, that we humans don't always know all the answers, and that we must constantly fight for restraint from our impulses to "help the wilderness along" or manage the wild out of wilderness.

It is because of the need for restraint and humility in our dealings with wilderness that Howard Zahniser, the author of the 1964 Wilderness Act, poetically defined wilderness as "an area where the earth and its community of life are untrammeled by man, where man himself is a visitor who does not remain." Zahniser, ever the meticulous wordsmith, intentionally chose the word "untrammeled" for this definition, meaning free from the control and manipulations of humankind. It is this word, more than any other in the Wilderness Act, that expresses the core meaning of "wilderness character," the phrase that resonates throughout the Wilderness Act.

In one of his many articles, Zahniser also aptly urged us to accept the role of "Guardians, Not Gardeners" when it comes to wilderness. Avoid the human impulse to manipulate, to garden, he meant, and instead guard the wilderness from manipulation. This, too, speaks to the intent of an untrammeled wilderness.

And a final thought. A quarter-century before this trip, when I was on an earlier canoe trip here in the Boundary Waters, a fire broke out near here and burned to the shores of Seagull Lake. I watched the firefighting planes fly overhead on their way to the fire from my spot far to the west and, when I climbed a high cliff and looked toward the fire, I saw the plume of smoke and a plane circling around it. The fire burned thousands of acres between Seagull and Saganaga, leaving blackened, charred ruins in its wake. I camped in the burn in the immediate years after the fire, interested in observing the forest regeneration, even though it left something to be desired in terms of aesthetics and beauty.

Today, we paddled past this same burn. A luxuriant and lush boreal forest now grows there, with nearly a quarter-century of renewal and growth. It is a beautiful forest now. It grew back from what was called a "devastating" fire that supposedly "destroyed" the forest, words more recently used to describe the windstorm as well. This new forest is also supple and limber. The recent windstorm affected it not one bit.

24

Care of Wilderness

Disturbing thoughts crowded my mind today as I paddled alone along the shores of a lake in the canoe country. Last night I spoke at a public hearing before four military officials. They proposed establishing a new low-level bomber training route over northeastern Minnesota for a variety of bombers, including the huge B-52. One segment of the proposed route crosses Superior National Forest to reach the military airspace where, supposedly at altitudes above 4,000 feet, fighter jets from Duluth would scramble to practice shooting them down. Already noise from the fighter jets, both afterburners and sonic booms, have shattered the great wilderness silences and solitudes of the canoe country. If we cannot stop the bombers, the canoe country will suffer a severe blow to its wilderness character.

Against this backdrop, and with these ominous thoughts weighing on my mind, I've arrived back in the Boundary Waters for an early May solo and the accompanying solitude.

Despite the early spring—the ice went out about April twentieth—the trees had not yet leafed out. Hillsides sat cloaked in their ethereal smoky mantles of delicate pale greens of aspen and the purple mauve blush of birch. Darker greens of spruce and pine stood out far more distinctly now than they will in another two weeks. These haunting hues of early spring in the north pass all too quickly, not fading but deepening in hue as leaves burst from buds and begin photosynthesis. One must be on time to see these shades in the spring, for they pass all too quickly in the rush toward summer.

I have come to Homer Lake in the Brule country, one of the lakes deserving of wilderness status and one that I and others have pressed the Forest Service to seriously recommend for wilderness in its various forest plans. I've come to more extensively explore Homer and Axe Lakes, to photograph their charms and beauty, and to explore the Vern River, the Pipe Lakes, and the Juno routes.

Homer Lake currently straddles the wilderness boundary—the eastern half lies outside the Boundary Waters Canoe Area Wilderness, the western portion within. The shores of Homer are marked by spruce and cedar stands meeting the shores of dark gabbro rock. Rock outcrops and slabs are present, and fifteen islands dot the lake's surface. Wildlife appears abundant. I see much beaver sign—lodges and peeled sticks—and common and hooded mergansers patrol the lake surface. Herring gulls and a bald eagle wheel overhead. The woods are full of the calling of white-throated sparrows, ruby-crowned kinglets, and the first of the yellow-rumped warblers.

I continued on my journey, exploring Homer Lake's limits, as well as those of Axe Lake, passing into the designated wilderness half of Homer. At the campsite near the west end I stopped to rest and take a nap. Then on through Whack Lake to Vern Lake I paddled, where I set up camp just east of the portage.

While preparing supper, I thought more about the proposed military flights above the wilderness. Stewardship came quickly to my mind. Wilderness stewardship encompasses a wide range of activities, from protecting wilderness character from intrusions by military jets, to proposing new areas to be added to wilderness, to maintaining the primitive campsites found within the BWCAW like the one at which I have camped. In my early years, I thought designating an area like the BWCAW was enough to protect it forever, but I have since learned that good wilderness stewardship is also vitally needed to protect the area in the long-term.

The Forest Service Wilderness Rangers who patrol in the BWCAW are among the most dedicated advocates of wilderness either within the agency or in wilderness advocacy organizations. I think of my friends, Rick Brandenburg and Ellen Hawkins, both of whom worked for many years in the Boundary Waters. Combining their years of service, they worked more than a half-century caring for the BWCAW. They worked hard at their wilderness stewardship responsibilities, maintained a pride and dedication in their work and to the wilderness, and usually received few accolades for their commitment or their tough physical work. Wilderness Rangers like Rick and Ellen are at the forefront of wilderness stewardship for the Boundary Waters.

Wilderness advocacy organizations also work on wilderness stewardship. They press for public policy decisions to protect wilderness areas, as many of us have done in opposing military flights above the Boundary Waters. Wilderness organizations also press the federal wilderness management agencies to do such things as limit administrative motor use within wildernesses, or use the least intrusive management options in carrying out their wilderness stewardship responsibilities.

The national wilderness conservation organization that best comprehends wilderness stewardship is the Montana-based Wilderness Watch. This organization deeply understands the purpose and intent of the Wilderness Act and the agencies' wilderness regulations, and presses all four federal wilderness administering agencies around the country to utilize the best wilderness stewardship practices to protect the wilderness character of all the units of the National Wilderness Preservation System. On occasion, organizations like Wilderness Watch must resort to the courts to seek their help in enforcing and interpreting the Wilderness Act directives for wilderness stewardship. Wilderness Watch is a great and spirited organization, and I'm proud to have served on Wilderness Watch's board of directors and now on the staff.

These ideas of wilderness stewardship filled my thoughts as I buttoned down my campsite for the evening. All of us who care about wilderness must continue to advocate for the best practices of wilderness stewardship nationally, for specific wildernesses, and very locally down to stewardship actions for specific portages and campsites. I crawled into my sleeping bag as darkness fell, reading until the light failed. Just to the west I heard the soft, winnowing call of a boreal owl. Though the challenges of wilderness stewardship remain, peace and solitude are mine tonight.

25

Bud's Fires

Today was our last full day of travel on this trip, going from Lac La Croix south to Nina-Moose Lake. We had a great trip so far, exploring some favorite places and enjoying late August swimming. It was time to start heading back, though, so we reluctantly began thinking of our return. We had an early start with an easy breakfast and a quick breaking of camp, and now were on the water paddling back to Boulder Bay.

We had a great treat in Boulder Bay shortly before the portage. Maja and I spotted a soaring bald eagle from a distance, then, as we turned around a point, Jean and Carlye spotted two eagles on the shoreline rocks. They were squawking and talking. As we neared, not just two, but three eagles took flight, one a speckled immature eagle. One of the adults had a fish in its talons. Off behind us and out of sight they flew. Then suddenly one adult and the young one flew back past us, and the young eagle took or stole the fish from the talons of the parent. They both then flew off into the trees and out of sight again, soon joined by the other adult.

We took the sixty-five-rod portage to the Boulder River, where Maja and Carlye each paddled in the stern across to the twenty-five-rod portage to Agnes Lake. Both girls have become accomplished paddlers.

Right here had been a ground fire among the tall pines almost fifteen years before. Now, young trees stood lush and thick underneath the tall pines.

My friend and mentor, Dr. Miron "Bud" Heinselman, had visited this site with his wife Fran just as the fire was burning itself out all those years ago. Bud was a world-renowned forest and fire ecologist for the Forest Service, whose research in the Boundary Waters did much to advance our understanding of the role of fire in this ecosystem over the centuries. Bud had argued for many years that fire played a natural role in the ecosystem, that it periodically renewed and regenerated the forests of the BWCAW. He had mapped the remaining areas of unlogged, virgin forest in the Boundary Waters (over half of the area), conducted field research to all corners of the Boundary Waters, and reconstructed the fire history of the Boundary Waters back to a fire in the year 1595 that had generated an old stand of red pines on Seagull Lake.

Bud reported on this Boulder Fire to the Forest Service, showing his attention to detail and understanding of fire ecology:

This fire was almost entirely a creeping, smoldering surface fire beneath old red and white pine. Red pine was most abundant on the ridges and steeper slopes, and white pine more abundant on lower slopes and in draws. The principal age classes of old pine were trees post-dating fires in 1681 and 1755-59, according to my earlier fire studies. The surface fires consumed varying amounts of the ground layer organic matter (duff) depending on slope position, aspect and probably soil variations, as well as overstory and understory species composition (which affects the character, arrangement, and flammability of the duff layer).

This area had obviously now regenerated from that surface fire, with young pines growing up where the fire had once burned.

Bud had also been deeply concerned with saving the Boundary Waters as a wilderness. He took an early retirement from the Forest Service and threw himself into the battles to save the BWCAW from logging, mining, and extensive motorized use. He and Fran helped form the Friends of the Boundary Waters Wilderness, Bud became its first chair, and he was at the center of the successful effort to pass the 1978 Boundary Waters Canoe Area Wilderness Act. The same passion that made him such an outstanding ecologist sustained him through that three-year effort to save the area he loved so deeply.

I stood there fondly remembering Bud as I gazed around at one of his Boundary Waters burns. We pushed on out into Agnes.

The weather continued hot and sunny the rest of the day as we paddled down Agnes Lake and the Nina-Moose River. We camped at a site on a point of land. I was reminded of another trip over twenty years ago, when I was finishing a week-long solo canoe trip in early May. As I was leaving Nina-Moose Lake on that trip, I unexpectedly ran into Bud and his friend George Collier, just starting out on a trip of their own. They invited me to join them for the night, so I turned my canoe around and began paddling back with them to the lake. Bud had pointed out to me a final peninsula on the right shore that contained older red pines that had survived the Little Sioux Fire about ten years before that. Interspersed among the living red pines were jack pines that had died in the same fire. Bud explained to George and me that jack pines were more susceptible to fires than red pines, and that each species of pine had its own strategies for surviving fires and regenerating itself. Bud, George, and I camped at the same campsite that night at which the four of us now stopped.

The next morning we broke camp, loaded the canoes, and headed across the lake and up the Moose River. I pointed out the peninsula to the girls, as Bud had done for me, where the Little Sioux Fire had burned long ago. Now a stand of thirty-year-old jack pines grew among the older red pines on that peninsula, the next generation taking its place in the forest.

26

The Musings of a
Springtime Solo

It rained much of the night, off and on, although never a heavy downpour. I listened long last night for saw-whet or boreal owls, but only heard spring peepers and frogs. This morning it is raining again, not very hard, but enough to make me want to stay in my sleeping bag a little while longer. The ruffed grouse are drumming in the woods, two loons swam by just off-shore, robins and white-throats call in the woods nearby.

The Boundary Waters country is so distinctive this time of year. Deciduous leaves have not yet unfolded now in early May, although the pale green aspen buds are bursting. The purple blush on shorelines marks the swelling buds of birch. Maple "flowers" have opened, and catkins of all sort abound.

The smells and scents of the North Woods, which upon first emergence from a car are always so delightful, fragrant, and intense, unfortunately become easily assimilated by my brain so that one almost loses awareness of their presence. The spicy spruce and balsam, the more subdued pine, the freshness of aspen. Balm of Gilead has such a strong, almost intoxicating fragrance as its buds are opening that it once woke me from a deep sleep. Ah, the smells of the Great North Woods!

It rained all day, and I chose to stay snug and warm in my bag except for brief forays outside. The wind picked up in the morning and has continued, at times quite strong. Many a time during the course of this day as the strong blasts of wind buffet my tent I have been glad I chose to stay put rather than travel. The wind and rain make the air seem much cooler outside than the temperature I measured here inside my tent.

I spent the day napping, snacking, reading, writing, and studying maps. Occasionally time will weigh a bit heavy, but not to the point of making me wish to break camp.

The sense of timelessness and freedom has been mine in full measure today. I never carry a watch in the wilds, and today the low, gray, overcast skies have made even rough estimates from the sun impossible. I read for a while, nap for a while, and never know if it's morning still or evening already. And of course it has made no difference in my day, as is proper in the woods. I sleep when tired, eat when hungry, and enjoy much time for thought, planning, and reflection. A most needed change of pace after too many months in the city.

The freedom that accompanies a solo trip in wild country is also evident today. By myself, with only my own plans and myself to worry about, I can hole up in the tent to ride out foul weather and not feel the need to move on due to another's hopes, goals, or expectations. I can change my travel plans at will, as I have done today, and alter my route as time, weather, and inclination have led me to do numerous times today. Although I love companionship,

I also relish the freedom that a solo trip can bring. If I want to go off exploring to a distant lake, I can. If I decide to push hard one day, I will. If I want to spend an hour or an entire morning photographing a special place, the choice is mine and mine alone.

The solitude that a solo trip brings is also a special part of a trip alone in the wilds. I am convinced that solo trips are not for everyone—not even for me most of the time—but if a person approaches such an experience with a proper frame of mind, such a trip can add great meaning to one's life. I am a fairly self-contained person, and can content myself with simple pleasures and the meanderings of my mind. I always obtain on these solo trips a heightened sense of awareness, and become absorbed in and by everything around me. This heightened awareness is at times so intense as to become almost intoxicating, something almost so joyful that every fiber of my body and mind seems vibrant and alive.

Solitude also brings time for thought, unhurried and unharried by schedules and distractions of civilized life. With such time and with no distractions of another person, thoughts come clearly and more easily to me. These in turn can bring reflection on life, work and activities, relationships with friends or family, and the mysteries and delights of life. Having another person along, even a close friend and like-minded companion, will diminish the timelessness, the freedom, and the solitude that can come best on a solo wilderness trip.

The rains and winds continue now even as the daylight begins to perceptibly fade. It is evening now, my first clue all day to the time, and I hope tomorrow's light will shine down through clear weather and blue skies.

27

Snowshoe Mission

I returned to Minnesota's Boundary Waters Canoe Area Wilderness for a late-winter snowshoe trip at the end of March. I went in to a small lake in the far eastern tip of the wilderness, one last visit in the snow before winter's grip on the land completely melted.

It was warm today, with no fear of frostbite, but the balmy temperatures have made the snow wet and dense. Snowshoeing— breaking trail in the soft wet snow—has been a challenge, but it should go easier tomorrow heading back out on the trail I broke today. There is still a good foot and a half of snow on the ground, and I sank down at least six inches with every step, even on snowshoes.

The snow looked a little tired and worn today at the end of winter. It has been melting, after all, and the surface shows needles, twigs, birchbark, cedar fronds, moose scat, and everything else. Gone is the fresh, clean white snow of early winter. Gone is the cold, crisp dry air of mid-winter. Winter is loosening its grip on the canoe country at last, after months of cold and snow and ice.

Now, as it nears dusk, I notice another sign of winter's retreat as I camp at the edge of Royal Lake. The Royal River is open and free of ice, and I just heard the whistling of duck wings flying along its length. It must be the first duck to return this early, and no doubt happy to find this stretch of open water amid all the snow and ice which, in another month, will all be gone. Royal

Lake, however, is still solid ice but for the channel of the river as it heads toward North Fowl Lake.

I've come to Royal Lake for a specific reason, too, beyond my usual reasons for visiting this fabulous wilderness. The U.S. Forest Service has proposed to build a new snowmobile trail on the imposing cliff rising 350 feet above the south shore of Royal Lake. It is an inane idea, one proposed to mollify snowmobilers from outside the wilderness who want a short route to nearby South Fowl and North Fowl Lakes for ice fishing.

For decades the snowmobilers had driven through Royal Lake and the BWCAW—illegally—to get to the Fowl Lakes. They had even developed and maintained a user-made trail, the so-called Tilbury Trail, that runs from McFarland Lake east to the Royal River and Royal Lake. It was on this trail that I snowshoed in.

I wanted to see Royal Lake and the cliff again, before any destruction had occurred on the cliff and before the wilderness character of Royal Lake had become forever damaged. The agency has been able to legally promote the proposed new trail because it would run just barely outside and above the wilderness boundary—but still within sight and sound of Royal Lake, within the BWCA Wilderness just below. Unfortunately, the Forest Service rejected several other trail alternatives that would have avoided impacts on Royal Lake and the wilderness.

Now, at dusk, it is completely still and quiet. Layers of fog hang over the open water of the Royal River. The only sound to reach my ears now as I stand outside my tent straining to hear is the distant murmur of the river as it leaves the lake and begins its tumble to North Fowl Lake. The great wilderness silences envelop me here as I stand alone, absorbed in the scene.

Quiet and silence are some of the prized attributes of a winter trip to the Boundary Waters, of trips to any wilderness in any season. They are increasingly rare as modern civilization, with its noise, machines, and impacts on the land, dominates more and more of the natural world. Wilderness areas like the Boundary

Waters offer the chance to experience wild country on its own terms, without sounds and sights and smells of civilization intruding. Quiet and silence are found in far greater abundance in the winter than in the summer in the canoe country, when the sounds of crowds often fill the lakes and woods. That's one of the reasons why the Forest Service snowmobile trail will damage the area's wilderness character.

Even though just outside the wilderness boundary, the raucous machines will destroy the peace and quiet, the sense of remoteness and detachment, to be found here. In the future, even if no snowmobile were to shatter the quiet on my next trip, just knowing that the trail exists and has damaged this magnificent cliff will lessen my experience and that of other visitors. And it would be such a senseless loss, when other trail alternatives would avoid diminishing the wilderness.

Must we continue down the path of this ill-advised trail?

I crawled into my tent. A cold rain fell all night.

28

The Mists of Brule Lake

We stood at the far west end of Brule Lake in the BWCA Wilderness, my two companions and I, looking toward the east through thick, dense fog. But for the gentle lapping of waves along the rock at our feet, silence ruled Brule Lake once again.

We had returned in May to this haunting wilderness lake in the canoe country, a lake finally freed of outboard motors. A provision of the 1978 BWCA Wilderness Act provided for the elimination of motorboats on Brule Lake by 1994, or until the one resort, located on the only parcel of privately owned shoreline on this large 5,200-acre lake, ceased operation. The resort owner requested a buy-out; the Forest Service complied and closed the lake to motors beginning in 1986. The agency later cleared the resort site and restored it to natural conditions.

BT, Dan, and I had returned in early May before others came back to visit the area. We had paddled long miles, hiked old trails, and explored some small, isolated lakes rarely seen by other travelers. Our long, circuitous route led us eventually to Brule and the mists that enveloped the lake.

The lake had itself returned, with wilderness conditions now restored, to a time before motorboats first came to Brule. Robert Marshall, the energetic wilderness champion and founder of the Wilderness Society in 1935, fought to preserve wilderness conditions on Brule Lake in the late 1930s. It was Marshall who, in one of his seminal wilderness articles in 1937, wrote this clarion call about the need for wilderness preservation: "Yet the universe of the wilderness, all over the United States, is vanishing with appalling rapidity. It is melting away like the last snowbank on some south-facing mountainside during a hot afternoon in June."

Marshall had canoed through the Quetico-Superior in 1937 with Sigurd Olson and, in his official capacity as chief of the division of recreation and lands in the U.S. Forest Service, struggled in early 1938 to keep Brule roadless and motorless.

In January of that year, at Marshall's urging, the Forest Service began formalizing its national wilderness classification system. As part of this process, local Forest Service officials had suggested deleting some land from the wilderness boundaries near Brule Lake and constructing an automobile road on an old logging railroad bed north to Brule.

Marshall strongly opposed this suggestion and responded immediately. "It would appear from the map," he wrote back, "that Brule Lake is the largest of the lakes entirely in United States territory which is not now accessible to automobile road. While I appreciate the desirability of another entrance into the primitive area, it is also true that there is a rare value, found, so far as I know, no place else within United States territory, of being able to camp on a lake as large as Brule Lake which is entirely free from any access by mechanized transportation."

A dead cedar arced gracefully up from the shoreline near us into the fog on the cool gray May morning. We sat and ate some lunch on this rocky shoreline, the natural sounds and silences enveloping us like the heavy fog that covered the land. Bob Marshall would have liked this day.

All those long years ago, the local foresters had written back to Marshall after his first letter, raising a new concern for the need for a road to Brule Lake. The territory around Brule and to the north was one of the worst fire areas in the entire forest, they claimed, and the most inaccessible for them to reach. They argued that five times within the past few years, they had to send over a hundred men to the Brule Lake country for fire suppression purposes. They wanted a road to Brule for firefighting. Marshall commonly heard about the supposed need for roads to aid fire-fighting as a reason to build roads into wilderness areas around the country.

Marshall fought on for the wilderness of Brule Lake through the maze of bureaucratic channels. He argued one more time for protecting Brule Lake, even with the proposed elimination of nearby lands from the primitive area boundaries. He insisted,

> Also I believe such an elimination should contain a con-tingent clause that no motorboats will be allowed on Brule Lake, except Forest Service motorboats which will be used only in fire emergencies. This would meet one of my two main objections to the elimination, namely, that it would destroy one of the very few opportunities in the country of camping on a large lake which is free from the noise of motorboats.

The waves continued to softly caress the shoreline after we fin-ished our lunch. We paced the fog-bound spot on Brule. Still the thick fog had not lifted. No foreign noises disturbed the lake now. A small tree-clad island just off shore faded in and out of sight in the heavy mists.

Unfortunately, Bob Marshall had lost his fight to keep Brule wild back in 1938, and with his early and untimely death in late 1939, he could no longer carry on his struggle within the Forest Service for this magical wilderness lake. The road came to Brule Lake, and motorboats became well established on the lake. But now, more than half a century later, Bob Marshall's dream for Brule Lake has been fulfilled. Motorboats have left Brule Lake forever, and wilderness conditions returned.

We stood at the western outlet of the lake as the mists and fog of Brule Lake swirled around us. The fog had not lifted; if anything, it had become more impenetrable. Should we wait until the dense fog lifted or venture out into the foggy unknown of the lake? We knew where we were heading, like Bob Marshall knew where he was heading half a century ago. And his dream had eventually come home to Brule.

Finally I pulled out my compass and we took a bearing into the formless fog bank. Out we paddled, into the mists of Brule Lake.

29

Faint Trails and Fading Light

We had pushed out into a small lake in the middle of nowhere. A cold autumn rain had fallen all afternoon. We had paddled back and forth several times along the western shoreline of this lake, looking for any signs of a faint trail or past human disturbance, knowing that would be the way out. Somewhere, we knew, a faint portage trail left this lake, if we could only find where it began.

Yet we had no luck. We hopped out of the canoe at several places along shore to search for tracks or sign, but could find nothing. Despite our rain gear, we were wet from both the rain and from bushwhacking through the dripping woods earlier in the day. The temperature had steadily dropped during the day's rain. And now we noticed that our daylight was fading fast.

BT and I had come back for a fall canoe trip together. We had had a great trip so far, with days of sunshine and rain, traveling through familiar country. Wolves howled all night long near one campsite, continuing on through the following morning. We paddled along rivers, past waterfalls, and through favorite lakes.

More than three decades before, during our guiding summers, we had each taken a group through this remote chain of small lakes, separated by long and rugged portages. Neither of us had journeyed there since. Current maps did not even show those old trails. But we wanted to see these lakes again, to travel through this remote country, to test our path-finding skills and old memories.

Earlier in the day, we had taken a couple of portages off the main route at the beginning of this chain of little lakes. Both portages were overgrown and brushy. A few deadfalls blocked the faint trail in places. It was obvious no one had traversed these trails in years. We stopped at a spot on one lake where people had camped years before. Should we stay here, or push on through the remaining lakes? We chose to push on, and our travels quickly became very challenging.

We had to hunt and hunt for the old portage out of that lake. We got out of the canoe in two different spots, trying to find the trail, but with no luck. Our memories from traveling through here long ago were of little help. We consulted our old maps again and paddled the shore further to the south. Finally we spotted it, overgrown by the shoreline growth. Exposure to ample sunlight there had helped the shoreline vegetation grow thickly in the years since any human visitor had passed through, concealing the old trail.

Once on the path, we could follow it through the woods fairly easily, despite the occasional windfall. Eventually the trail appeared to end at a swampy channel, which we surmised might lead to the next lake beyond. The old maps showed the portage skirting this lowland to the south, but we could see no trail continuing anywhere from that point. We decided to try paddling the swamp in hopes we could make it to the next lake. After some hopping in and out of the canoe to pull it over logs in the swamp, we finally made it to the lake as the rain began to fall.

From this little lake, we needed to find a half-mile portage to the next lake. Locating this trail proved the most difficult yet. We split up, bushwhacking along the shores in opposite directions, hoping one of us would cut across the trail. After two such attempts, we still hadn't found the portage as the rain steadily increased. Finally BT cut across the trail back in the woods, followed it back to the lake where it descended steeply to the shore, and I paddled the canoe over to this now completely indiscernible portage landing.

Off we trudged in the rain, with the woods, trail, and rocks quite wet by this time. It was a long, slow slog, but we kept going until we finally reached the swampy shore of the next small lake.

The next half-mile portage we found fairly easily, since it started on a more upland piece of shoreline. Again we took our time on this carry, trying to be careful of the wet woods and slippery trail. Finally we reached the lake on which we now found ourselves at another swampy indiscernible portage ending.

We paddled back and forth along the shoreline several times, cutting through the woods in search of one last faint trail. We were wet, hungry, and quickly running out of daylight. We needed to improvise quickly. I suggested we try a little shelf of rock back near where we had entered the lake. We found no room back of the rock for a tent as I had hoped, but we pitched the tent atop the tiny shelf itself and bivouacked for the night, cold, wet, hungry, and cramped for space.

Despite these circumstances, we had had a great day. We had safely made our way through remote country, found and followed disappearing trails, bivouacked safely for the night in the middle of nowhere. One must always be prepared to travel through wilderness on its terms, its conditions, and its nature. Our years of travel in the Boundary Waters continue to teach us this lesson.

Recently the field of conservation biology has explored the concept of rewilding lands and landscapes. This concept usually refers to restoring wildness to a large expanse of land through ecological restoration, removal of roads, returning top carnivores, and so forth. But on a much smaller scale, BT and I had discovered that this small route in the Boundary Waters Wilderness had been rewilded over the past three decades—wilderness improved not by trail crew work but by increased wildness and a lack of human traffic.

Though the Boundary Waters remains too crowded on many routes during the summer, this chain of lakes at least is much wilder than it was more than three decades ago. It felt nice to discover this restored wildness, and by two old guides still capable of threading our way through the backcountry.

A beaver splashed on our small lake all night. The next day, we would finally find our last faint trail in more rain and wind and cold, hidden along the edge of the cranberry bog. We were physically spent, but reveled nonetheless in our day of faint trails and fading light.

30

Wilderness Trail

I shared a trail one day in the Boundary Waters, not with another person, but with a moose. It had come by earlier in the day and left its large cloven prints in the mud and duff. I came by much later, near sunset, after spending the day exploring a lake and the large waterfall that fed it, near a place that had once threatened the wild character of this land years ago.

After a long winter away, I had returned to the canoe country north and west of Lake Superior. I had come in early May by myself to capture the feel of the land just after the break-up, to gaze down the long vistas of a special lake that haunts my memory, and to experience the pure joy of wilderness travel by canoe. I had done these things and more, and now had begun to head back, satisfied with this time in my favorite land now empty of humankind.

The water stood high in the lakes so soon after the melt, and the shorelines of the lakes I paddled had flooded, glaciated spits of rock had submerged and shoreline trees and shrubs were left standing in water. As I neared the portage landing, the low western sun glaring in my eyes, the familiar spot had gone—the rocky shelf and tiny curve of sand had disappeared. Had I not crossed this spot several times before, I would have remained perplexed, but suddenly realizing the inundated situation I began paddling my canoe inland between the flooded alder and hazel brush. After nearly ten-rods, I saw my portage trail rise out of the water in front of the canoe.

Since this portage trail ran a long distance—a mile in length— and my one large pack weighed considerably, I decided to split the load and carry it as the French voyageurs had done—in *posés* or half-mile segments. I set off with my pack through the aspen and spruce woods. Immediately I saw the tracks of the moose. We were the first to walk the trail this spring, the moose and I, for only our tracks disturbed the surface of the trail. I stopped a moment to examine a particularly distinct track in the mud. The moose was large, I thought, perhaps a big bull, and had walked this trail just earlier in the day. As the trail wound through a stand of aspen, the level rays of the sun highlighted every track the moose had left in the disturbed leaves on the trail. Finally I came to a good stopping point near an old beaver flowage, and I dropped the pack to return for the canoe.

I soon returned to my pack with the canoe and discovered around the corner that the trail—normally passable at this point— ran into standing water. The moose tracks disappeared under the water. I loaded the pack in my canoe and began paddling along the "trail," now several feet below my canoe. An eerie feeling came over me as I paddled along, trying to remember where the trail led among the tall, branchless dead snags that had drowned long ago. Red-winged blackbirds flew noisily at my approach, surprised by the intrusion. A pair of blue-wing teal swam quickly away.

Then, near the far end of the standing water, I heard sloshing in the water. As my canoe glided soundlessly closer, at last I could see the source of the noise—the moose from the trail! He fed in the shallows, a large bull around six feet tall at the shoulder and weighing perhaps a half-ton. His antlers had not yet grown much this early in the season, each velvet-covered antler about fifteen inches long and completely horizontal, with a palmate knob at each end.

Inadvertently I made a small noise and suddenly alerted the moose, with his keen sense of hearing, to my presence. We both froze, motionless, the moose and I, waiting to see what the other would do. For long minutes we stood that way, he in the water and I in the canoe.

At long last the moose began moving off, breaking the tense silence with his sloshing. As he reached a more distant spot he turned to eye me once more. First he snorted, then bellowed—not once but four times, as if to show his displeasure with my interruption. Our meeting noisily terminated, the moose headed through the swamp to the north and I returned to paddling the trail.

The sun had set now, and as I paddled ahead trying to pick out the trail through the flooded dead trees, my thoughts jumped ahead to the campsite I wanted and the routine chores awaiting me there: pitching my tent on the carpet of needles under the tall red pines, preparing and eating a simple supper, and luxuriating in the sounds and smells of another evening in the canoe country.

During this time out I had caught the rhythms of the land during the excitement of early spring, had shared my quiet and solitude with moose and warblers, bald eagles and beavers. I had visited places of great beauty and hidden history, and had captured a feel for the battles this land had seen. I mused on and searched the dusk for signs of the flooded trail.

As I peered through the fading light I realized that my experience on the trail today reflected much of the long history of the efforts to protect the canoe country. At times during the past century the route to long-term preservation of the area has been level and straight, at other times flooded with threats, at still other times fraught with conflict and confrontation. Though we have made great progress over the course of that trail, a great distance yet remains before we find the humility and exercise the restraint to grant the Boundary Waters the full wilderness protection it so richly deserves, free from motorized intrusions of all kinds, safe from all threats, and preserved as a rich wild, untrammeled legacy for all generations.

At last I found the portage emerging from the waters of this embattled wilderness and landed the canoe where the trail climbed to dry ground. I grunted as I threw the canoe to my shoulders and stared ahead at the long uphill path before me. How far must this path go? My goal awaited me in the dusk on the far side; I headed up the trail.